ARCO
Literary Critiques

Charlotte and Emily Brontë

Norman Sherry, Ph.D.

arco
New York

Acknowledgements

The author and publishers are indebted to the National Portrait Gallery for permission to reproduce the portraits on the cover. The diary fragment written by Emily Brontë is reproduced by kind permission of The Brontë Society. The engraving of The Clergy Daughters' School at Cowan Bridge is reproduced by kind permission of the Headmistress of Casterton School.

For my brothers Tom and Alan

Published 1970 by ARCO PUBLISHING COMPANY, Inc.
219 Park Avenue South, New York, N.Y. 10003
Copyright © Norman Sherry, 1969, 1970
All Rights Reserved
Library of Congress Catalog Number 73-101773
Printed in the United States of America

Arco Literary Critiques

Of recent years, the ordinary man who reads for pleasure has been gradually excluded from that great debate in which every intelligent reader of the classics takes part. There are two reasons for this: first, so much criticism floods from the world's presses that no one but a scholar living entirely among books can hope to read it all; and second, the critics and analysts, mostly academics, use a language that only their fellows in the same discipline can understand.

Consequently criticism, which should be as 'inevitable as breathing'—an activity for which we are all qualified—has become the private field of a few warring factions who shout their unintelligible battle cries to each other but make little communication to the common man.

Arco Literary Critiques aims at giving a straightforward account of literature and of writers—straightforward both in content and in language. Critical jargon is as far as possible avoided; any terms that must be used are explained simply; and the constant preoccupation of the authors of the Series is to be lucid.

It is our hope that each book will be easily understood, that it will adequately describe its subject without pretentiousness so that the intelligent reader who wants to know about Donne or Keats or Shakespeare will find enough in it to bring him up to date on critical estimates.

Even those who are well read, we believe, can benefit from a lucid exposition of what they may have taken for granted, and perhaps—dare it be said?—not fully understood.

K. H. G.

Charlotte and Emily Brontë

In this book I have dealt with the published novels of Charlotte and Emily Brontë and with the poems of Emily. I have tried to show the importance of the close family circle of the Brontës as the area from which their imaginative work stemmed, and the influence upon their work of their reading, and also of those limited aspects of Victorian life in which they were involved.

In the case of Charlotte, having considered her prentice work, *The Professor*, I have gone on to trace the development of her achievement of a personal voice in *Jane Eyre* and *Villette*, and her failure in *Shirley* to move from personal to social concerns. In the case of Emily I have included a short chapter on her poetry, and two long chapters on her remarkable novel, *Wuthering Heights*. In these chapters the paradox of the discrepancy between her life and experience and her literary achievement has been a major concern, as has been also the Shakespearian quality of her novel, and the nature of 'reality' as it appears there. Anne Brontë's work has been treated only incidentally, but I have attempted to show her standing in relation to the works of her two sisters.

There are so many editions of the novels of the Brontës that it was thought more convenient to give chapter references for quotations rather than page numbers. The bibliography at the back of the book gives the main works of criticism that have appeared.

I should like to express my appreciation for the assistance of Professor Kenneth Muir and Dr. Miriam Allott in reading the book at manuscript stage, and to the General Editor of the Series, Kenneth Grose, for his very valuable and willing assistance throughout.

N. S.

Contents

The Author

Norman Sherry, B.A., Ph.D., is Senior Lecturer in English Literature at the University of Liverpool. He is author of *Jane Austen* in this series and of *Conrad's Eastern World* (Cambridge University Press).

Jane Eyre

by Currer Bell

vol. I.

Chap. 1st

There was no possibility of taking a walk that day.
We had been wandering indeed in the leafless shrubbery
an hour in the morning, but since dinner (Mrs Reed,
when there was no company, dined early) the cold winter
wind had brought with it clouds so sombre, a rain so pen-
etrating that further out-door exercise was now out of the
question.

I was glad of it; I never liked long walks — especially
on chilly afternoons; dreadful to me was the coming home
in the raw twilight with nipped fingers and toes, and a heart
saddened by the chidings of Bessie, the nurse, and humbled
by the consciousness of my physical inferiority to Eliza, John
and Georgiana Reed.

The said Eliza, John and Georgiana were now clustered
round their Mamma in the drawing-room; she lay reclined

The first page of the manuscript of *Jane Eyre*

A diary fragment written by Emily Brontë on 26 June 1837

The Clergy Daughters' School at Cowan Bridge

I

Their Lives and Writings

An old gamekeeper of the Haworth area is reported, in 1897, to have said that he didn't believe in Charlotte Brontë: 'She never wrote those books they talk about . . . poor waik little thing—some gentlefawks met and boxed them up for her.' This reflects something of the general attitude to the Brontë sisters. The contemporary reaction to their novels, ranging from the enthusiastic to the shocked, was powerful, and was enhanced by the later revelation that they were the work of inexperienced spinsters. The novels, particularly those of Emily and Charlotte, had the same vivid and emotional impact as had the story of their lives, and for this reason, no doubt, the interest in the two has always developed together.

The tendency to link the fictional world with its author is seen as early as 1849, when Charlotte first met Thackeray at a dinner-party. As the gentlemen entered the drawing-room after dinner, he asked her 'if she had perceived the scent of their cigars'; to which she replied literally, discovering in a minute afterwards, by the smile on several faces, that he was alluding to a passage in *Jane Eyre*. In Chapter 23 of the novel, Jane, in the garden at Thornfield, is warned of Rochester's presence by 'a subtle, well-known scent—that of a cigar' stealing from some window.

'All true histories contain instruction', wrote Anne Brontë in *Agnes Grey*. It would be difficult to say what instruction we should draw from the 'true history' of the Brontë family unless we were to accept Charlotte's own words, quoted by Mrs. Gaskell in her biography, on the subject of life:

> She [Charlotte] said in her own composed manner, as if she had accepted the theory as a fact, that she believed some were appointed

beforehand to sorrow and much disappointment; that it did not fall to the lot of all—as Scripture told us—to have their lines fall in pleasant places; that it was well for those who had rougher paths to perceive that such was God's will concerning them, and try to moderate their expectations, leaving hope to those of a different doom, and seeking patience and resignation as the virtues they were to cultivate . . . there was some good reason, which we should know in time, why sorrow and disappointment were to be the lot of some on earth.   MRS. GASKELL, Chapter XXVII

Sorrow, disappointment, and early death were the doom of all the Brontë children, but we notice that Charlotte uses the phrases 'it was well for', 'try to moderate their expectations', 'seeking patience and resignation'. Charlotte, Branwell, Emily and Anne were involved in a constant struggle with their fate and at the same time a yearning to come to terms with it. Each member of the family found an individual solution to the problem. Emily withdrew into stoicism and mysticism, Anne turned to religion and resignation, Charlotte developed a determined perseverance, and Branwell found relief in drink and drugs.

HAWORTH

In 1853, when she was thirty-seven, Charlotte Brontë wrote to Mrs. Gaskell inviting her to visit Haworth. She apologised for the place having no attractions, apart from the moors—'the sole but, with one who loves nature as you do, not despicable resource': '. . . the heath is in bloom now: I have waited and watched for its purple signal as the fore-runner of your coming. It will not be quite faded before the 16th, but after that it will soon grow sere.'

Mrs. Gaskell recorded, in her biography of Charlotte of 1857, her impressions of the Brontë home, Haworth Parsonage in Yorkshire. She describes the 'four tough, steep scrambling miles' from Keighley to Haworth, 'the road winding between the wave-like hills':

Haworth is a long, straggling village: one steep narrow street—so steep that the flag-stones with which it is paved are placed end-ways that the horses' feet may have something to cling to, and not slip

> down backwards . . . we . . . reached the church . . . then we turned
> off into a lane on the left . . . up to the parsonage yard door . . .
> moors everywhere beyond and above. Chapter XXVII

> The house is of grey stone, two stories high, heavily roofed with
> flags . . . [it consists] of four rooms on each story; the two windows
> on the right . . . belonging to Mr. Brontë's study, the two on the
> left to the family sitting-room. Chapter I

It was to this parsonage that, in April 1820, the Reverend
Patrick Brontë brought his wife and family of young children.
'There are those yet alive,' wrote Mrs. Gaskell in her biography,
'who remember seven heavily-laden carts lumbering slowly up
the long stone street, bearing the "new parson's" household goods
to his future abode.' In one of the carts were, presumably, the six
Brontë children, all under seven years of age: Maria (born in
1813), Elizabeth (1815), Charlotte (1816), Patrick Branwell
(1817), Emily Jane (1818), and Anne (1820).

Patrick Brontë, then forty-three, came of poor Irish parents in
County Down, his father's name being Brunty which Patrick
later changed to Brontë. By effort and determination, and in the
face of great poverty, he got himself to Cambridge and was
ordained in 1806. Before settling at Haworth he had held various
curacies, and had married Maria Branwell, a Cornish woman, in
1812. He was the author of several books of poetry and sermons.

The Brontës' life at Haworth began with a tragedy. Mrs.
Brontë fell ill in January 1821, and died in the September troubled
by the thought of her young children left without her. The
household was afterwards managed by her sister, Miss Elizabeth
Branwell, who left her home in Penzance to live at Haworth, but
never reconciled herself to the barren Yorkshire moors, the
climate, and the stone floors of the parsonage.

The Brontë children were discouraged from mixing with the
Haworth children and hence led a comparatively isolated existence. Patrick Brontë valued his privacy and cherished it. Because
of a digestive trouble, he took most of his meals alone in his study,
his time being spent in that room when he was not out on parish
business. Increasingly also, Miss Branwell kept to her own room,
eventually giving the girls their lessons there.

The woman who came to nurse Mrs. Brontë in her last illness told Mrs. Gaskell how the six children would take their walks together—on the moors, rather than towards the village—hand in hand. ' "You would not have known there was a child in the house, they were such still, noiseless, good little creatures. Maria would shut herself up" (Maria, but seven!) "in the children's study [a narrow room above the hall] with a newspaper, and be able to tell one everything when she came out; debates in Parliament, and I don't know what." ' (Mrs. Gaskell, Chapter III).

COWAN BRIDGE SCHOOL

In 1824, Maria and Elizabeth were sent to the Clergy Daughters' School at Cowan Bridge, not far from Kendal, and Charlotte and Emily soon followed them. Maria was then ten, Emily only six.

The school was partly a charity school, and the fees were small —£14 per year, with accomplishments such as music or drawing £3 extra each. The pupils wore 'plain straw cottage bonnets; in summer, white frocks on Sundays, and nankeen on other days; in winter purple stuff frocks, and purple cloth cloaks'. The Reverend William Carus Wilson was prime mover in the founding of the school, which opened in 1824, and mainly in charge of it.

The discipline was rigorous, the teaching harsh; the food was inadequate, badly cooked, and often stale; and many of the girls must have suffered from cold and fatigue when, on winter Sundays, they walked two miles to church and ate their cold lunch between services in the unheated church.

Maria Brontë had always been delicate, and these conditions proved too much for her. Her life at school was not made easier by the persecution of one teacher who took a dislike to her. She developed tuberculosis and was sent home in February 1825, to die less than three months later at the age of eleven.

Many of the girls at Cowan Bridge meanwhile went down with a low fever, and, a few weeks after Maria's death, Elizabeth was also brought home sick. Charlotte and Emily do not seem to have been affected by the fever, but Mr. Brontë decided to bring them home also. Elizabeth died only two weeks after returning to Haworth.

The impressions made upon Charlotte by these experiences at Cowan Bridge were never to be forgotten, and they produced the early chapters of *Jane Eyre* in which she revered the memory of her sister in the character of Helen Burns and condemned the Reverend Carus Wilson and the teacher who persecuted Maria in the characters of Mr. Brocklehurst and Miss Scatcherd.

At the age of nine, Charlotte was now the eldest of the family, and took Maria's place in looking after the younger children. At this time, they found a new friend in a Yorkshire woman who came as servant to the family—Tabitha Ackroyd, known to them as 'Tabby', rough, shrewd, practical, but kind and devoted to the family. She was to be with them until she died a few months before Charlotte.

ANGRIA AND GONDAL

Mr. Brontë saw signs of rising talent in his children even before the tragic Cowan Bridge episode, though the records of that school do not remark on such talent, recording only the weaknesses of the education the Brontë girls had received from their father and aunt.

The true genius of the children was to show itself, not in terms of formal academic achievement, but in the acting and recording of certain original plays whose existence was kept a strict secret. It is from Charlotte's accounts that we learn of this rich imaginative life of the Brontë children. She recorded, when she was thirteen, the origin, in 1827, of their play, 'The Islanders':

> One night, about the time when the cold sleet and stormy fogs of November are succeeded by the snow-storms, and high piercing night winds of confirmed winter, we were all sitting round the warm blazing kitchen fire, having just concluded a quarrel with Tabby concerning the propriety of lighting a candle, from which she came off victorious, no candle having been produced. A long pause succeeded, which was at last broken by Branwell saying, in a lazy manner, 'I don't know what to do.' This was echoed by Emily and Anne.
>   '*Tabby.* "Wha ya may go t'bed."
>   '*Branwell.* "I'd rather do anything than that."

'*Charlotte.* "Why are you so glum tonight, Tabby? Oh! suppose we each had an island of our own."
'*Branwell.* "If we had I would choose the Isle of Man."
'*Charlotte.* "And I would choose the Isle of Wight."
'*Emily.* "The Isle of Arran for me."
'*Anne.* "And mine shall be Guernsey." '

Another note of Charlotte's called 'The History of the Year 1829' describes how their father's gift of some toy soldiers to Branwell began the play of the 'Young Men'. Each of the children seized a soldier and gave him a name—Charlotte's was the Duke of Wellington, Emily's Gravey, Anne's Waiting-Boy, and Branwell's Bonaparte. The 'Young Men' were settled in the land of the Ashantees (the Gold Coast), and there established the kingdom of Angria.

It was from these plays that the Brontë juvenilia sprang. The accounts of their imaginary kingdoms, the exploits and tragedies of their leaders, their feuds and battles and loves were written down in minute print on tiny pages—the smallest is an inch and a half long—and stitched together and covered with wrapping paper from the Haworth shops. More than a hundred of these tiny volumes still exist.

The Brontë children would seem to have lived more in their imaginary kingdoms of Angria and Gondal than in the real world—Charlotte and Branwell being eventually responsible for the Angria saga, Emily and Anne for the Gondal saga. But the actual world, particularly the political and literary events of the time, played its part in their games, as their choice of heroes shows. Wellington and his two sons, Napoleon, Leigh Hunt, Walter Scott, Lord Bentinck, Christopher North, editor of *Blackwood's Magazine*, all appear in these fictional worlds.

The grip of this imaginary world upon Charlotte is shown by an entry in her diary when she was twenty and a teacher at Roe Head School. Her escape from the unpleasantness of her life was to lose herself completely in visions of Angria, the violent Gothic and Byronic world of handsome, amoral, passionate and sadistic aristocrats. On this occasion she wrote:

Never shall I, Charlotte Brontë, forget . . . how distinctly I, sitting in the schoolroom at Roe Head, saw the Duke of Zamorna leaning against that obelisk . . . I was quite gone. I had really, utterly forgot where I was . . . I felt myself breathing quick and short as I beheld the Duke lifting up his sable crest, which undulated as the plume of a hearse waves to the wind . . . 'Miss Brontë, what are you thinking about?' said a voice, and Miss Lister thrust her little rough, black head into my face.

And when, in 1845, Emily and Anne went together for a trip to York, they imagined themselves to be Gondal characters during the excursion.

ROE HEAD

In January 1831, when she was almost fifteen, Charlotte was again sent to school—Miss Margaret Wooler's school at Roe Head, near Huddersfield. Mary Taylor, a pupil at the school, gave this description of her on her arrival:

I first saw her coming out of a covered cart, in very old-fashioned clothes, and looking very cold and miserable . . . She looked a little old woman, so short-sighted that she always appeared to be seeking something . . . She was very shy and nervous, and spoke with a strong Irish accent.

From her year at Roe Head, Charlotte gained two firm friends— Ellen Nussey and Mary Taylor, an interest in the Luddite riots from Miss Wooler, improved education, and an even stronger urge to educate herself and her sisters, so that they could get on in life. She returned to Haworth to study by herself, to teach her sisters, as well as to take up again her share of the household duties.

Although it is generally from Charlotte's writings that we obtain insight into the Brontë family life, Emily left some scraps of writing that give us vivid pictures of the family as well as evidence of Emily's observant eye and sense of humour. On 24 November 1834, when Emily was sixteen, she wrote:

Anne and I have been peeling Apples for Charlotte to make an apple pudding and for Aunts nuts and apples Charlotte said she made puddings perfectly and was of a quick but lim[i]ted intellect Taby said just now Come Anne pilloputate (i.e. pill a potato) Aunt has come into the kitchen just now and said where are your feet Anne Anne answered On the floor Aunt papa opened the parlour door and gave Branwell a letter saying here Branwell read this and show it to your Aunt and Charlotte—The Gondals are discovering the interior of Gaaldine Sally Mosley is washing in the back-kitchin

It is past Twelve o'clock Anne and I have not tid[i]ed ourselves, done our bed work or done our lessons and we want to go out to play we are going to have for Dinner Boiled Beef Turnips, potatoes and apple-pudding . . . Tabby said on my putting a pen in her face Ya pitter pottering there instead of pilling a potate I answered O Dear, O Dear, O Dear I will directly with that I get up, take a knife and begin pilling . . .

TEACHERS AND GOVERNESSES

In July 1835 Charlotte wrote a letter to Ellen Nussey which marked the beginning of some years of change in the lives of the family:

> We are all about to divide, break up, separate. Emily is going to school, Branwell is going to London, and I am going to be a governess. This last determination I formed myself, knowing that I should have to take the step sometime . . . and knowing well that papa would have enough to do with his limited income, should Branwell be placed at the Royal Academy, and Emily at Roe Head . . . I am going to teach in the very school where I was myself taught. Miss Wooler made me the offer, and I preferred it to one or two proposals of private governess-ship . . .

The pattern of their lives for the next ten years was thus established. Until 1845 the three Brontë sisters went out, at intervals, into the world as teachers, governesses, and as students. Aware that Branwell, who was to be a painter, must, as the only son, be given his chance, they realised that they must get on by their own efforts. There was not money enough for the education of all four of them. The girls must earn their own livings and be independent.

In those days, such independence could be gained by girls in their situation only by becoming governesses or teachers. Teaching, in either form, never appealed to the Brontës. Their natural shyness, the strong bonds of home, their inability to cope with pupils, or at least to feel much sympathy for them, set up strains which nearly always brought about nervous illnesses.

Anne was perhaps the most persistent in keeping to her path in life where earning her living by teaching was concerned. Charlotte always suffered eventually, but Emily could least of the three remain from home for very long.

> Liberty was the breath of Emily's nostrils; without it she perished. The change from her own home to a school, and from her own very noiseless, very secluded, but unrestricted and inartificial mode of life, to one of disciplined routine . . . was what she failed in enduring. Her nature proved here too strong for her fortitude . . . In this struggle her health was quickly broken . . .
>
> MRS. GASKELL, Chapter VIII

And so, Emily returned to Haworth after only three months as a pupil at Roe Head and her place was taken by Anne. To play her part in their plan, however, Emily made up by taking on the cooking and much of the housework at Haworth.

BRANWELL'S FAILURE

But Branwell's part in the scheme of 1835 was a complete failure. He made his trip to London to seek admission to the Academy Schools, and spent some days there, but does not appear to have gone near the Academy, nor to have delivered the letters of introduction with which he was provided.

Branwell was not without talent, as his writing and paintings show, but no doubt both he and his sisters had come to imagine that talent greater than it was. Charlotte said of him that 'Nature had favoured him with a fairer outside, as well as a finer constitution, than his sisters.' His aunt spoiled him, and his father, allowing him greater freedom than his sisters, was not aware of how he spent his leisure time. He mixed with the people of Haworth, and was much admired by them for his wit and intellect. He was often sent for to the Black Bull Inn in the village to entertain visitors with his conversation. It was the dangers of this greater freedom that Charlotte had in mind when she compared how girls were carefully kept from experience while 'boys are turned loose on the world as if they, of all beings in existence, were the wisest and least liable to be led astray'.

A note written by Anne on Emily's birthday, 1841, reflects the unsettled and uneasy existence of the sisters as governesses:

> Four years ago I was at school. Since then I have been a governess at Blake Hall, left it, come to Thorp Green, and seen the sea and York Minster. Emily has been a teacher at Miss Patchett's school, and left it. Charlotte has left Miss Wooler's, been a governess at Mrs. Sidgwick's, left her, and gone to Mrs. White's. Branwell has given up painting, been a tutor in Cumberland, left it, and become a clerk on the railroad.

As a result, they developed their cherished idea of setting up their own school eventually, so that they might at least live and work together and as their own mistresses. And from this came Charlotte's more ambitious plan for furthering their education. She wrote to her aunt in 1841:

> My friends recommend me, if I desire to secure permanent success, to delay commencing the school for six months longer, and by all means contrive, by hook or by crook, to spend the intervening time in some school on the Continent . . . I would go to Brussels . . . living is there little more than half as dear as it is in England, and the facilities for education are equal or superior to any other place in Europe . . . I could improve greatly in Italian, and even get a dash of German . . .

In 1842 Charlotte and Emily, accompanied by Mr. Brontë and Mary Taylor and her brother, went to Brussels and became pupils at the Pensionnat Heger in the Rue d'Isabelle, where the schoolrooms and dormitories, the garden with the 'allée défendue' were as Charlotte was later to describe them in *Villette*. Madame Heger ran the Pensionnat, while her husband was professor at the Athénée Royal de Bruxelles. The sisters stayed there until November 1842 when they were called home as a result of their aunt's illness and death.

To people who knew them in Brussels, they were a strange pair:

> The two sisters clung together and kept apart from the . . . Belgian
> girls . . . Emily had taken a fancy to the fashion, ugly and prepos-
> terous . . . of gigot sleeves, and persisted in wearing them long after
> they were 'gone out'. Her petticoats, too, had not a curve or a wave
> in them, but hung down straight and long, clinging to her lanky
> figure. The sisters spoke to no one but from necessity . . . During
> the hours of recreation . . . they invariably walked together, and
> generally kept a profound silence . . . Charlotte would always
> answer when spoken to . . . Emily rarely spoke to anyone.
>
> MRS. GASKELL, Chapter XI

Friends in Brussels who invited them out, were eventually
totally discouraged:

> Emily hardly ever uttered more than a monosyllable. Charlotte
> was sometimes excited sufficiently to speak eloquently and well—
> on certain subjects; but before her tongue was thus loosened she had
> a habit of gradually wheeling round on her chair so as almost to
> conceal her face from the person to whom she was speaking.
>
> MRS. GASKELL, Chapter XI

This self-imposed isolation stemmed from their shyness, their
strangeness, and their strong religious convictions. Charlotte's
letters to Ellen reveal her true opinions. Brussels is 'a great
selfish city' and the Pensionnat 'a great selfish school'. The
national character of the Belgians is 'singularly cold, selfish,
animal, and inferior . . . My advice to all Protestants who are
tempted to do anything so besotted as turn Catholics, is, to
walk over the sea on to the Continent; to attend mass sedulously
for a time; to note well the mummeries thereof; also the idiotic,
mercenary aspect of all the priests . . .'.

But M. Heger took an interest in the sisters, had some understanding of their unusual nature and genius, and gave them
private lessons in French. Charlotte wrote of him:

> He is professor of rhetoric, a man of power as to mind, but very
> choleric and irritable in temperament; a little black being, with a
> face that varies in expression. Sometimes he borrows the lineaments

of an insane tom-cat, sometimes those of a delirious hyena; occasionally, but very seldom, he discards these perilous attractions and assumes an air not above 100 degrees removed from mild and gentleman-like.   Letter to Ellen Nussey, May 1842

In 1843 Anne returned to Thorp Green taking Branwell with her to work as tutor to the son of the Robinson family, Emily remained at home, and Charlotte returned to the Pensionnat in Brussels as a teacher.

She suffered an even greater isolation and loneliness, for Madame and Monsieur Heger became reserved and cold towards her. She wrote: 'I get on here from day to day in a Robinson-Crusoe-like sort of way, very lonely.' In 1844 she left Brussels and arrived at the parsonage on 23 January.

It would seem that Charlotte was struggling with some kind of hopeless passion for Monsieur Heger—perhaps the reason for Madame Heger's coldness towards her. Certainly her letters to him in the following years suggest something of the sort.

The following year Anne and Branwell returned from Thorp Green, and the family were reunited, but under unhappy circumstances. Anne wrote in July 1845, '. . . during my stay [at Thorp Green] I have had some very unpleasant and undreamt-of experiences of human nature'. She was doubtlessly referring to Branwell's passion for Mrs. Robinson, which eventually resulted in his dismissal from Thorp Green. The incident seems to have broken him entirely. 'He was very ill on Thursday,' Anne records, '. . . we hope he will be better and do better in future.' But Branwell's decline was steady from that point. He drank increasingly, took opium, and was constantly borrowing and in debt.

> I went into the room where Branwell was, to speak to him, [wrote Charlotte to Ellen Nussey] about an hour after I got home; it was very forced work to address him. I might have spared myself the trouble, as he took no notice . . . he was stupefied . . . he had got a sovereign from papa . . . he went immediately and changed it at a public-house, and has employed it as was to be expected. Emily concluded her account by saying he was a hopeless being; it is too true . . . What the future has in store I do not know.

But it was during this period of stress and unhappiness that the sisters made their first attempt to publish their work.

> One day, in the autumn of 1845, I accidentally lighted on a MS. volume of verse in my sister Emily's handwriting. Of course, I was not surprised, knowing that she could and did write verse . . . I thought them condensed and terse, vigorous and genuine . . . it took hours to reconcile her to the discovery I had made . . . Meantime, my younger sister quietly produced some of her own compositions . . . We agreed to arrange a small selection of our poems, and, if possible, get them printed. Averse to personal publicity, we veiled our own names under those of Currer, Ellis, and Acton Bell . . . . 'Biographical Notice of Ellis and Acton Bell' by Charlotte Brontë, 1850.

The poems were published by Messrs. Aylott and Jones of Paternoster Row about the end of May 1846, at the expense of the authors. In the year following publication, only two copies were sold.

But in one of her letters to their publisher, Charlotte had made the following comment: 'C., E. and A. Bell are now preparing for the press a work of fiction, consisting of three distinct and unconnected tales, which may be published either together, as a work of three volumes, of the ordinary novel size, or separately as single volumes.' These tales were *The Professor*, *Wuthering Heights*, and *Agnes Grey*, and by 1846 they were going the round of the publishers, first together and then separately, without any success.

At this time, Mr. Brontë's eyesight was giving the sisters increasing anxiety, and in August Charlotte went with him to Manchester so that his eyes might be operated on. Charlotte told Mrs. Gaskell that encouraged by a courteous letter from the publishers, Smith, Elder & Co., she began, at this time, when she was with her father in lodgings in Manchester, another novel— *Jane Eyre*.

THE NOVELS

In the early summer of 1847, *Wuthering Heights* and *Agnes Grey* were accepted for publication by Mr. Newby of Mortimer Street, 'on terms somewhat impoverishing to the two authors'. But for the time being, Newby made no attempt to bring the novels out.

While they waited for news of these, Charlotte's *Jane Eyre* was accepted by Smith, Elder & Co. and was published by them on 16 October 1847.

The impact of the novel was immediate, and finds its reflection most strongly in the reaction of private individuals to it. George Smith, head of the firm that published it, began reading it one Sunday morning and put off engagements and meals until he finished it that same evening. Thackeray also complained that he lost a whole day reading it. Thackeray's daughter Anne records being 'carried away by an undreamed of and hitherto unimagined whirlwind into things, times, places, all utterly absorbing' in reading the book. 'I heard no news [at Mrs. Sydney Smith's] except great praise of *Jane Eyre*', records a contemporary.

Charlotte was persuaded by her sisters to let her father into her secret, which she did, leaving him with a copy of the novel. When he came into the parlour for tea, he said, 'Girls, do you know Charlotte has been writing a book, and it is much better than likely?'

No doubt spurred on by the success of *Jane Eyre*, Newby now brought out the novels of Emily and Anne in December 1847, and thus their year of success ended for the Brontë sisters.

But in the following year, Newby, in trying to sell Anne's second book, *The Tenant of Wildfell Hall*, in America, expressed the opinion that all the novels were the work of one writer. Rightly or wrongly, Charlotte felt that the mystery about the authorship of the novels should be cleared up with her publisher, and Charlotte and Anne started for London to reveal their identity to Smith, Elder & Co. After breakfast, bewildered by London and exhausted by the journey, they set out for the publishing house:

> On reaching Mr. Smith's, Charlotte put his own letter into his hands ... 'Where did you get this?' said he, as if he could not believe that the two young ladies dressed in black, of slight figures and

diminutive stature, looking pleased yet agitated, could be the
embodied Currer and Acton Bell . . . MRS. GASKELL, Chapter XVI

They returned to their inn, the Chapter Coffee House, Paternoster Row, and Charlotte suffered from a racking headache
and sickness as a result of the excitement. In spite of their wishes
not to be known or taken about, the sisters were taken to the
Opera, the Royal Academy, and the National Gallery, and dined
at Mr. Smith's house:

> On Tuesday morning we left London, laden with books Mr. Smith
> had given us . . . A more jaded wretch than I looked . . . it would be
> difficult to conceive. I was thin when I went, but I was meagre
> indeed when I returned; my face looking grey and very old, with
> strange, deep lines ploughed in it—my eyes stared unnaturally.
> Letter from Charlotte Brontë to Mary Taylor, 4 September 1848

THREE DEATHS

Their brief moments of success were to be followed by months
of sickness and tragedy, during which three of the Brontës
died, leaving Charlotte to face life alone.

In July, Charlotte wrote of her brother, 'Branwell is the
same in conduct as ever. His constitution seems much shattered.
Papa, and sometimes all of us, have sad nights with him.' And
some idea of his desperate state can be gained from a letter
written by Branwell, one Sunday in 1848, to his friend, the
sexton at Haworth:

> Dear John,
>   I shall feel very much obliged to you if [you] can contrive to get
> me Five pence worth of Gin in a proper measure.
>   Should it be speedily got I could perhaps take it from you or
> Billy at the lane top, or, what would be quite as well, send out for,
> to you.
>   I anxiously ask the favour because I know the good it will do me.
>   *Punctually* at Half-past Nine in the morning you will be paid the
> 5d. out of a shilling given me then,—Yours, P.B.B.

Branwell, whose hopes and talents had once seemed equal to
those of his sisters, was now in no state to enter into their success.
On 9 October Charlotte wrote:

23

The past three weeks have been a dark interval in our humble home. Branwell's constitution has been failing fast all the summer; but still neither the doctors nor himself thought him so near his end as he was. He was entirely confined to his bed but for one single day, and was in the village two days before his death. He died after twenty minutes' struggle, on Sunday morning, September 24th.

So ended what she called his 'brief, erring, suffering, feverish life', and such was the end of the early hopes they had all had for him.

It was the cold and cough Emily took at his funeral that was to bring on the second tragedy in so short a time. On 29 October Charlotte wrote:

Emily's cold and cough are very obstinate. I fear she has pain in her chest, and I sometimes catch a shortness in her breathing when she has moved at all quickly. She looks very thin and pale . . . It is useless to question her; you get no answers. It is still more useless to recommend remedies; they are never adopted.

Emily sank rapidly. She refused all help, would not see a doctor. Her stern independence caused her sisters much heartache. One morning, having dressed and taken up her sewing, it was apparent to them that she was dying. At last she gasped, 'If you will send for a doctor, I will see him now.' At two o'clock, she died.

Charlotte's fears were now for Anne, who had never been strong, and was now found to be suffering from tubercular consumption. Charlotte, watching her growing worse, wrote: 'These things would be too much if reason, unsupported by religion, were condemned to bear them alone.' In May, hoping to do her some good, Charlotte took Anne to Scarborough, Ellen Nussey accompanying them, but the change did not help. She died on 28 May, and was buried in Scarborough.

Charlotte stayed a few weeks in Scarborough before returning to the parsonage.

CHARLOTTE ALONE

Of her first night at the parsonage, Charlotte wrote: 'So the sense of desolation and bitterness took possession of me. The agony that *was to be undergone*, and *was not* to be avoided, came on. I underwent it, and passed a dreary evening and night, and a mournful morrow; to-day I am better.' But she could not get over the loss and the loneliness:

> The great trial is when evening closes and night approaches. At that hour we used to assemble in the dining-room—we used to talk. Now I sit by myself—necessarily I am silent . . . My life is what I expected it to be. Sometimes when I wake in the morning, and know that Solitude, Remembrance, and Longing are to be almost my sole companions all day through . . . sometimes . . . I have a heavy heart of it.

In spite of her grief and loneliness, she retained the will to go on with her work: 'But crushed I am not, yet . . . I have some strength to fight the battle of life . . . Still I can *get on.*'

She took up again the writing of *Shirley*, a novel begun before her sisters' deaths. For subject, she had gone back to Miss Wooler's stories at Roe Head of the Luddite riots—riots her father had experienced at first hand; for the character of Shirley herself she took her sister Emily; and for various other characters, she looked to her acquaintances—the curates were modelled on the curates of Haworth.

Shirley was published in October 1849, again under the pseudonym of Currer Bell. In spite of Charlotte's desire to remain unknown, a Haworth man living in Liverpool, who recognised the places described in the book, suspected she was the authoress and published his suspicions in a Liverpool paper. And when Charlotte visited London at the end of 1849, she was received as the authoress of *Jane Eyre*.

From this time, Charlotte's life took on a different character. At Haworth there was still the loneliness, the fears for her own health and that of her father. But her fame as a novelist had spread to Haworth; the Mechanics Institute ordered *Shirley*, and lots were drawn to see who should borrow the volumes first. She made visits to London, Scotland, and the Lake District, as well as to the homes of friends. She met Thackeray, Harriet Martineau, and Mrs. Gaskell.

The reissue of *Wuthering Heights* and *Agnes Grey* caused her to write a Preface for the volume and a memoir of her sisters, and she was also at work on *Villette*. On one visit to London she heard Thackeray lecture and saw a performance by the actress Rachel—a performance which found its place in her last novel. *Villette* was completed in 1852 and appeared early in 1853. It was received with acclaim, and Charlotte wrote: 'The import of all the notices is such as to make my heart swell with thankfulness to Him who takes note both of suffering, and work, and motives. Papa is pleased too.'

It was at this time—in December 1852—that she received a proposal of marriage most unexpectedly. She had in earlier years rejected three such proposals. In reply to one she had written: '. . . I will never, for the sake of attaining the distinction of matrimony and escaping the stigma of an old maid, take a worthy man whom I am conscious I cannot render happy.'

The Reverend Arthur Bell Nicholls had been her father's curate in Haworth since May 1845, when Charlotte had written of him, '. . . Papa has got a new Curate lately, a Mr. Nicholls from Ireland . . . he appears a respectable young man . . .' And now, in December 1852, she wrote to Ellen Nussey:

> On Monday evening Mr. Nicholls was here to tea. I vaguely felt without clearly seeing, as without seeing, I have felt for some time, the meaning of his constant looks, and strange feverish restraint. After tea I withdrew to the dining-room as usual. As usual, Mr. Nicholls sat with papa till between eight and nine o'clock. I then heard him open the parlour door as if going. I expected the clash of the front door. He stopped in the passage: he tapped: like lightning it flashed on me what was coming.

Opposition to their marriage came from Mr. Brontë: 'Papa's vehement antipathy to the bare thought of any one thinking of me as a wife, and Mr. Nicholls's distress, both give me pain.' Mr. Nicholls left Haworth, but Charlotte corresponded with him, and Mr. Brontë's consent was obtained in April 1854. The small, flagged passage room behind Charlotte's study was converted into a study for Mr. Nicholls, and they were married on 29 June.

Charlotte's married life was to be a brief one. She visited Ireland with her husband, and then they returned to the parsonage: 'Since I came home, I have not had an unemployed moment; my life is changed indeed, to be wanted continually, to be constantly called for and occupied seems so strange,' she wrote to Ellen Nussey on 9 August. But in November she caught a cold which considerably weakened her, and in the new year she was very ill. The illness was pronounced to be only part of her pregnancy, but it increased, she had a high fever, was bilious and could neither eat nor sleep. Tabby, their old servant, died at this time, and Charlotte lived only until March. She also was buried in Haworth graveyard.

Her father and husband lived on together until Mr. Brontë's death in 1861 at the age of eighty-four when Mr. Nicholls retired to Ireland and remarried.

2

Background and Influences

Isolation is the idea conjured up initially by the Brontës' life, isolation of a geographical, social, and intellectual kind. Certainly Haworth Parsonage was remote in those days—the eight-mile journey from Bradford took the Brontë family a whole day when they first travelled to Haworth. And for the girls of the family, apart from their association through the church, there could be no intercourse with Haworth society. In childhood, the effect of this was to intensify the family life and the imaginative activity of the children. Her friend Mary Taylor told Charlotte they were 'like growing potatoes in a cellar'.

This kind of life no doubt accounted for the extreme shyness of Charlotte and Anne, and what Mrs. Gaskell preferred to see in Emily as reserve. It limited their experience of society and social behaviour. At the same time it fostered individualism in outlook and opinion, and probably also an intense emotional response to life. Charlotte's reaction to her first view of the sea was described by Ellen Nussey: 'As soon as they were near enough for Charlotte to see it in its expanse, she was quite overpowered; she could not speak until she had shed some tears . For the remainder of the day she was very quiet, subdued, and exhausted.'

But the Brontës did not suffer total isolation. It was not isolation from literature. Charlotte's letter to Ellen Nussey on 4 July 1834 gives us some idea of the wide and enthusiastic reading interests of the family:

> If you like poetry, let it be first-rate; Milton, Shakespeare, Thomson, Goldsmith, Pope (if you will, though I don't admire him), Scott, Byron, Campbell, Wordsworth, and Southey. Now don't be

startled at the names of Shakespeare and Byron. Both these were great men, and their works are like themselves. You will know how to choose the good, and to avoid the evil; the finest passages are always the purest, the bad are invariably revolting; you will never wish to read them over twice. Omit the comedies of Shakespeare, and the *Don Juan*, perhaps the *Cain*, of Byron, though the latter is a magnificent poem, and read the rest fearlessly; that must indeed be a depraved mind which can gather evil from *Henry VIII, Richard III*, from *Macbeth*, and *Hamlet*, and *Julius Caesar*. Scott's sweet, wild romantic poetry can do you no harm. Nor can Wordsworth's, nor Campbell's, nor Southey's—the greatest part at least of his . . . For history read Hume, Rollin, and the *Universal History*, if you *can*: I never did. For fiction, read Scott alone; all novels after his are worthless. For biography, read Johnson's *Lives of the Poets*, Boswell's *Life of Johnson*, Southey's *Life of Nelson*, Lockhart's *Life of Burns*, Moore's *Life of Sheridan*, Moore's *Life of Byron*, Wolfe's *Remains*. For natural history, read Bewick and Audubon, and Goldsmith and White's *History of Selborne*.

Charlotte was eighteen when she wrote this, and it therefore represents her interests at an early age. It is presumably not intended as exhaustive, but as a list of recommended reading—those authors she then regarded as best. It implies a moral censorship, on the principle that what is best is pure, and it reveals two strong influences on the Brontës, Scott's historical novels and poetry, and the poetry and life of Byron. Both of these writers influenced the Brontës, first through their Gondal and Angrian sagas, and then through their novels. It was those aspects of exile, violence and romantic love in the life of Byron that impressed them.

The reading of the Brontë sisters was, of course, much wider than this, including German and French literature, and, judging from references in Charlotte's novels, such books as the Gothic novels of Mrs. Radcliffe, Richardson's *Pamela, The Arabian Nights, Gulliver's Travels*, Bewick's *Book of British Birds*, Johnson's *Rasselas*, and old copies of the *Ladies' Magazine* belonging to their aunt, and her 'mad methodist magazines'.

Nor were the Brontës isolated from political and religious events of the day. The strong interest in politics which dated from their earliest years has already been mentioned. It was fed by the newspapers that came regularly into the parsonage. Charlotte wrote in 1829: 'We take two and see three newspapers a week. We take the *Leeds Intelligencer*, Tory, and the *Leeds Mercury*, Whig . . . We see the *John Bull*; it is a High Tory, very violent. Mr. Driver lends us it, as likewise *Blackwood's Magazine*, the most able periodical there is . . .' But it was fed also by discussion of current events and of past history among the family and friends. One of Charlotte's schoolfellows at Roe Head school recorded: 'We used to be furious politicians, as one could hardly help being in 1832. She knew the names of the two ministries; the one that resigned, and the one that succeeded and passed the Reform Bill. She worshipped the Duke of Wellington, but said that Sir Robert Peel was not to be trusted.'

This interest in politics, religion and military matters must have come initially from their father. While Mr. Brontë was at Cambridge, Napoleon's army was massing at Boulogne, and England was faced with the threat of invasion. He joined the corps of volunteers, and became expert in the handling of the latest weapons. When he escorted Charlotte and Emily to Brussels, he visited the field of Waterloo, and afterwards described it in one of his sermons.

In 1809 he was curate at Dewsbury in Yorkshire, where there was already talk of installing labour-saving machines in the mills. There was discontent in the area which was to break out in the violence of the Luddite Riots. At Heartshead in 1812, very near to Roe Head where Charlotte was later to go to school, Mr. Brontë was in the midst of frame-breaking disturbances that had spread northward from Nottingham. It was at this time that he took to carrying pistols with him whenever he went out.

While Patrick Brontë was at Dewsbury, he saw also the splitting off from the Anglican church of the Methodist movement and the setting up of independent Methodist churches. Both Patrick and Miss Branwell were supporters of the Evangelical movement, though Patrick remained faithful to the established church.

Nor were they isolated from certain strong, personal, emotional experiences. The influence of nature as it appeared in the loneliness and wildness of the moorland, linked them inevitably with the Romantic Movement which undoubtedly was a strong influence in their lives. At different times, Charlotte and Branwell corresponded with Wordsworth, Southey, and Hartley Coleridge. The sisters sent copies of their book of poems to Wordsworth, Tennyson, Lockhart, and De Quincey.

Whatever the nature of Charlotte's feeling for Monsieur Heger, it brought her the experience of strong admiration and of affection that was rejected. And Branwell's unhappy love for Mrs. Robinson with its disastrous results in his own degradation was part, inevitably, of the experience of his sisters. Charlotte, after hearing Thackeray lecture on Fielding, objected that she would never let a brother of hers read his lecture because of his light way of dealing with Fielding's 'character and vices': 'Had Thackeray owned a son, grown, or growing up . . . would he have spoken in that light way of courses that lead to disgrace and the grave? . . . I believe, if only once the prospect of a promising life blasted on the outset by wild ways had passed close under his eyes, he never *could* have spoken with such levity of what led to its piteous destruction.' She obviously had Branwell's wasted life in mind.

Thus the intimate experiences of their family life are an important source and influence for the Brontës.

EXPERIENCE OF THE WORLD—TEACHING

Nor were they entirely without experience of the world beyond Haworth, though it was experience of a specific kind. Their work as teachers and governesses brought them into contact with certain aspects of contemporary society.

The Brontës were part of a historical situation which was reflected in the literature of the time. The rise of a wealthy middle class—mainly the *nouveaux riches* manufacturers—produced employers for the number of impoverished gentlewomen, often daughters of clergy, who could impart not only an education but some idea of manners and deportment. The position of these women in wealthy houses was frequently ambiguous. Their duties might include sewing, dressmaking and acting as nursery maids. Charlotte records: 'Mrs. Sidgwick . . . overwhelms me with oceans of needlework, yards of cambric to hem, muslin nightcaps to make . . . dolls to dress.'

The average salary in the 1840s and 1850s was thirty to forty guineas a year. Agnes Grey, the heroine of Anne's first novel, is offered a salary of £25 per annum by her first employer, which is presumably the salary Anne received at Blake Hall. Charlotte, at her last post as governess, was paid £20 per annum, but the cost of her laundry was deducted from this. The Robinsons later paid Anne £50 per year.

A concern for the plight of governesses brought about the formation of the Governesses' Benevolent Institution in 1841, and an interest in the governess is revealed in the literature of the time. The situation of a poor girl of good family forced to earn her living in this way, or by teaching in a school, appears, of course, in the Brontës' novels—in *Agnes Grey*, *Jane Eyre*, *Shirley*, *Villette*, *The Professor*.

The Brontës' situation here reminds us of Jane Fairfax in *Emma* (1816), who was also to go out and earn her living as a governess, a fate which is described as retiring 'from all the pleasures of life, of rational intercourse, equal society, peace and hope, to penance and mortification for ever'. In 1839 Harriet Martineau's novel *Deerbrook*, with its figure of the solitary governess, was published; the down-trodden Miss Pinch appeared in *Martin Chuzzlewit* in 1843; the wicked and scheming Miss Becky Sharp in *Vanity Fair* in 1848, to mention only a few of the varieties and numbers of governesses who made their appearance in the fiction of the time.

The alternative to teaching in a family was to teach in a school, which Emily and Charlotte both did, but found it little less onerous than being governesses. For this reason, the idea of having their own school appealed so much to the sisters. They had before them the example of Miss Wooler's establishment at Roe Head. But to open a school they needed further educational qualifications. And obtaining such qualifications was no easy matter for women at that time. In 1847 a series of Lectures to

Ladies was begun in London, and certificates of proficiency were granted. The following year Queen's College for Women was founded, whose classes were attended at one time by George Eliot. The aim of these projects—to enable women to equip themselves better for teaching—shows the contemporary awakening of an interest in the education of women, and even Tennyson deals with it in his poem *The Princess* of 1847.

TEACHING EXPERIENCE AND THE NOVELS

So strong was the influence of their teaching experiences upon the Brontës that we find in their novels many passages dealing with the contemporary attitude to teachers and governesses, and passages revealing the inadequacies of the sisters as teachers. Even in the romantic *Jane Eyre*, we have a solid tract on education. The initial scenes with Helen Burns show the business of teaching from the pupil's point of view. But Jane as governess overhears the following conversation about governesses:

> I have just one word to say of the whole tribe; they are a nuisance. Not that I ever suffered much from them; I took care to turn the tables. What tricks Theodore and I used to play [on our governesses] —spilt our tea, crumbled our bread and butter, tossed our books up to the ceiling, and played at charivari with the ruler and desk, the fender and fire-irons. Chapter 17

Passages of *Agnes Grey* reveal Anne's inadequacy as a teacher, and the difficulties she encountered:

> I had to run after my pupils to catch them, to carry or drag them to the table, and often forcibly to hold them there till the lesson was done. Tom I frequently put into a corner, seating myself before him in a chair, with a book . . . in my hand . . . he would stand twisting his body and face into most grotesque and singular contortions . . . and uttering loud yells . . . Mary Ann . . . would drop like a leaden weight; and when I, with great difficulty, had succeeded in uprooting her thence, I had still to hold her there with one arm, while with the other I held the book . . .

Lucy Snowe, in *Villette*, takes a firmer hand with her pupils, even shutting one into a cupboard, and so quells them.

33

But the governess or teacher was peculiarly well situated for obtaining a view of human nature when the veils of politeness and convention had been withdrawn. Both Jane Eyre and Agnes Grey are made to feel the nothingness of a governess's position by people who ought to have known better and who, by their attitude, reveal a faulty nature. Agnes Grey is ignored, even by the local clergyman:

> ... he would persist in putting them up and closing the door, till one of the family stopped him by calling out that the governess was not in yet; then . . . he departed . . . leaving the footman to finish the business.
>
> Nota bene.—Mr. Hatfield never spoke to me, neither did Sir Hugh nor Lady Meltham, nor Mr. Harry . . . nor any other lady or gentleman who frequented that church: nor any one that visited at Horton Lodge.

And further indications of human nature are revealed to Agnes Grey in young Tom's cruelty to animals, and in her older pupils' treatment of the poor, and the mercenary and flirtatious attitude of Miss Murray.

Charlotte, summing up her experiences to Mrs. Gaskell, said 'that none but those who had been in the position of a governess could ever realise the dark side of "respectable" human nature; under no temptation to crime, but daily giving way to selfishness and ill-temper, till its conduct towards those dependent on it sometimes amounts to a tyranny of which one would rather be the victim than the inflicter' (Mrs. Gaskell, Chapter VIII).

Primarily, in the novels of both Anne and Charlotte therefore, the teacher is a judge of the moral character of her pupils and colleagues, and such moral character is seen as the result of upbringing and education. Adèle Varens, in *Jane Eyre*, is an ordinary child with no 'deficiency or vice'—'and no injudicious interference' thwarts Jane Eyre's plans for her improvement. So she became obedient and teachable. Agnes Grey finds that her pupils, indulged or neglected by their parents, are disobedient, ignorant, cruel, even unprincipled. Lucy Snowe watches with disapproval Madame Beck's reaction to her daughter Désirée's vicious behaviour. Even in *Wuthering Heights*, the idea of the need for education, discipline and control is present. Cathy and Heathcliff 'both promised fair to grow up as rude as savages; the young master being entirely negligent how they behaved, and what they did'. Rochester compares himself with Jane—she 'a girl well reared and disciplined', he 'a wild boy indulged from childhood upwards'.

The strongest, if harshest, example of the precept that a child's upbringing prepares him for life is in the *Tenant of Wildfell Hall*, when Helen Graham explains that her little son Arthur 'detests the very sight of wine . . . and the smell of it almost makes him sick. I have been accustomed to make him swallow a little wine or weak spirits and water, by way of medicine when he was sick, and, in fact, I have done what I could to make him hate them'.

This is not to see the Brontë novels as tracts on the right education and upbringing of children so that they can face the world as adults and not fall into sin; but the conception of human nature as imperfect and likely to fall into wrong paths unless provided with the necessary principles which will assist the individual to make the right choices in life is a strong undertow to the novels.

EXPERIENCE OF THE WORLD—PUBLISHING

The Brontës' experience of this aspect of contemporary social concern was felt at a very personal level. And as novelists they also broke through their isolation to a contact with the outside world, and another contemporary bone of contention where women were concerned.

The demand for novels from the circulating libraries provided the opportunity for a woman at home to support herself by writing if she had the knack—and many did, though there were objections also to women as writers. Southey, replying to Charlotte's request for advice, wrote: 'Literature cannot be the business of a woman's life, and it ought not to be . . . The more she is engaged in her proper duties, the less leisure will she have for it.' In 1852 George Lewes asked lady novelists: 'Does it never strike these delightful creatures that their little fingers were made to be kissed not to be inked? . . . Are there no stockings to darn, no purses to make, no braces to embroider? *My* idea of a perfect woman is one who can write but won't.'

The Brontës inevitably came up against this question of whether writing and publishing were properly a woman's concern, though Charlotte seems to have been most incensed by the attitude to women novelists: 'I wished critics would judge me as an *author*, not as a woman,' she wrote to Lewes.

It was held by many that if a woman *must* write, she should limit her subject-matter to seemly situations and emotions. Thus the Brontë novels were all found to be 'coarse', and *Jane Eyre* was thought, by one reviewer, to have been written by 'one who has, for some sufficient reason, long forfeited the society of her own sex'.

The Brontës chose to publish at first under pseudonyms, and they took male names for their purpose. This might have been a hangover from Angrian and Gondal days; it might have been a desire to remain anonymous in Haworth. But it was also, almost certainly, related to the contemporary attitude towards women writers.

Thus, in spite of a certain kind of isolation, the Brontës had sufficient experience of contemporary concerns and their novels share, to some considerable degree, the interests which appear in contemporary novels. Apart from stories already mentioned about governess life, Disraeli's *Sybil* and Mrs. Gaskell's *Mary Barton* were concerned with social conditions and the working poor, as was *Shirley*. The centring of a novel's interest in a child, as in parts of *Jane Eyre* and *Wuthering Heights*, had been done by Dickens. Novels of high-life, known as productions of the 'silver-fork school', had been very popular, and *The Tenant of Wildfell Hall* is partly of this kind. But novels of middle-class and low life were becoming popular, as was the introduction of a specific geographical setting, often regional, with a strong sense of place.

The moral concern of a novel was also of prime importance. Maria Edgeworth's novels, still popular then, were strongly moral, and it is in this lack of a specific moral that the Brontë novels upset their first readers. Critics attempted to place novels in accordance with their didactic themes, and *Jane Eyre*, in one instance, was seen as 'warning to all placed in authority over the young, whether in the capacity of parent, teacher or nurse . . . against leaving the young and impressible in the charge of un-educated and lax-principled servants'. *Wuthering Heights* was condemned for lacking social or moral aim.

But the Brontës did not write novels in order to illustrate a particular moral precept. Such an obvious procedure is deliberately rejected at the end of *Shirley*: 'I think I now see the judicious reader putting on his spectacles to look for the moral. It would be an insult to his sagacity to offer directions. I only say, God speed him in the quest!'

THEIR INDIVIDUALISM

Although in certain respects related to the contemporary novel, therefore, the Brontës' novels nevertheless were found to be different. One effect of isolation upon their works would seem to be an individuality and originality of response to experience which offended readers since it resulted in an unusually open and honest—or naïve—treatment of such things as love, profligacy and violence. There was a certain sense of things set down without reference to what was expected and accepted, and an individual approach to life that enabled them to see familiar and commonplace things as new and strange. Something of the kind of impact their novels made is shown in the remark of one lady who, after reading them, thought she would rather visit the Red Indians than trust herself in Leeds.

That the Brontës themselves saw nothing unusual in their novels and were puzzled and hurt by condemnation of them, is shown in Charlotte's Preface to the 1850 edition of *Wuthering Heights*: 'I have just read over *Wuthering Heights*, and, for the first time, have obtained a clear glimpse of what are termed (and, perhaps, really are) its faults; have gained a definite notion of how it appears to other people . . .'

ANNE BRONTË

Anne Brontë's novels are little read today. Anne lacked that genius of her sisters which enabled their work to carry over its interest from one generation to another. They are limited in terms of insight, of characterisation, and in conception of theme. They are much more firmly rooted in the immediate and prosaic concerns of her life and of her time and of the literature of her time, and to that extent belong to the minor novels of the period. They will not, therefore, be treated in detail in this book, but it is useful to consider them in conjunction with the novels of Charlotte and Emily—they provide a point of similarity and of comparison. Anne, who, though the youngest, always the weakest physically of the sisters, and very retiring, nevertheless spent so much time struggling as a governess, produced novels which are most obviously, in form and theme, related to contemporary literature. Even then, however, they have that freshness at times which comes from the innocence of a person writing who has known nothing of the sophistication of society. Thus, Charlotte wrote of *The Tenant of Wildfell Hall*, 'The choice of subject was an entire mistake. Nothing less congruous with the writer's nature could be conceived . . . She had, in the course of her life, been called on to contemplate, near at hand and for a long time, the terrible effects of talents misused and faculties abused . . . she believed it to be a duty to reproduce every detail . . . as a warning to others.' The close observation of her brother's affair with Mrs. Robinson and his subsequent degeneracy were the events which so impressed Anne. And in this sense, her experience of life was probably more unusual and more painful than that of many others who lived in a wider society. Her naïveté combined with her strong reactions to Branwell produced the novel intended to reveal the dangers of drink and immoral living, and strong though the moral sense is, it forced her to reproduce scenes of debauchery with unerring detail and truthfulness. Similarly, *Agnes Grey*, though it is like other governess stories, takes its freshness of observation from Anne herself, and its lack of structural and artistic skill from her own lack of sophistication.

CHARLOTTE BRONTË

Charlotte was much more in the world than the others, and her increasing contact with it on a variety of planes is revealed in her

novels. *Jane Eyre*, though it moves over ground
interest such as charity schools and their abuses,
of governesses and teachers, is the work still of
aware of herself or of these issues as part of a wic
it is the individual and isolated passion of Jane 1
anger at injustice and cruelty, her temptation t(
and religion for individual happiness, her see
independent mode of existence. The univ(
approaches that of *Wuthering Heights* in th(
individual's reaction to its own moral ambience and emotional
universe. But this was not solely Charlotte's sphere for she was
not the isolated spirit Emily was. The position of women, the
fear of being an old maid, the struggle for independence on the
world's terms, not by retreat to the spiritual, make *Shirley* and
Villette novels based more firmly in a recognised society. They
deal with problems of the individual seen more and more in
relation to society, while still revealing an individual vision.

EMILY BRONTË

Emily had less contact with the world beyond the parsonage than
any of them. 'My sister's disposition was not naturally gregarious,'
writes Charlotte with magnificent understatement. 'Though her
feeling for the people round was benevolent, intercourse with
them she never sought; nor, with very few exceptions, ever
experienced. And yet she knew them: knew their ways, their
language, their family histories; she could hear of them with
interest, and talk of them with detail, minute, graphic, and
accurate; but *with* them she rarely exchanged a word.' That such
seclusion produced *Wuthering Heights* is not in itself exceptional.
Material for such a novel was at hand even for a recluse. The ways
of the Yorkshire people about her must have been part of her life,
and tales of their lives and adventures must have come readily
through gossip of the servants, etc. into the parsonage. 'On the
moors,' wrote Mrs. Gaskell, 'we met no one. Here and there in
the gloom of the distant hollows she pointed out a dark grey
dwelling . . . and told me such wild tales of the ungovernable
families who lived or had lived therein that *Wuthering Heights*

ed tame comparatively.' Together with such tales, had the inspiration of reading and the imaginative freedom ondal. Her novel is strange, again because of that lack of oncern with the standards beyond her 'world', standards which could not view the events of *Wuthering Heights* as calmly or with the moral acceptance of Joseph or Nelly Dean; standards which prevented, at that time, a writer from presenting certain matters as they were. But it was such unsophistication and naïveté in worldly matters which allowed her to present these people completely within the fictional world, untrammelled by any sense of their being unusual. Emily did not see her world in relation to moral or social concerns of the day. She was not irked by the restrictions placed on women in society, and presumably viewed Branwell's self-destruction as the action of a free soul going its own way—as did Heathcliff and Hindley and Cathy. She was able to see such events, she observed the reasons for certain actions, but she was so removed from the influence of everyday morality that she did not need to judge, or to point a warning lesson. Her comment on Branwell was that he was 'a hopeless being', but she does not seem to have felt any of the moral disgust for him that Charlotte felt.

This attitude is responsible for lifting the universe of *Wuthering Heights* beyond the limitations of the contemporary moral world to a wider belief in the basic qualities of human nature. Such matters as education or lack of it, the role of woman in society and her relationship with men, the social reaction to the effects of degradation, are not her concern. In certain instances, human nature survives in its virtues in spite of degradation; on the other hand, a fierce passion can create unhappiness for itself and others that strikes across the social and moral codes of society, but brings misery which is spiritual; and again a weak nature crossed by unhappiness, and without the stabilising effect of standards, can ruin itself.

The individualism of the Brontës is therefore a varied and not a static thing. It is based on isolation, it is based on an original and personal viewpoint as a result of isolation, but it varied with each of them according to her nature and experience.

3

The Professor

The Professor, although the first of Charlotte Brontë's novels to be written, was the last to be published. It appeared in 1857, two years after her death. When a second attempt to get it published after the appearance of *Shirley* was unsuccessful, Charlotte put it away. Some of the material on which it is based—her experiences at the Pensionnat Heger in Brussels—was re-worked later in *Villette*.

The authoress of *Jane Eyre* began her first novel with what appear to be uncharacteristic working principles:

> 'I said to myself that my hero should work his way through life as I had seen real living men work theirs—that he should never get a shilling he had not earned—that no sudden turns should lift him in a moment to wealth and high station; that whatever small competency he might gain, should be won by the sweat of his brow . . . that he should not even marry a beautiful girl or a lady of rank.'

Thus, in the preface to *The Professor*, Charlotte Brontë laid down the limits of her novel—limits confining her to realism in terms of action, and her hero to poverty and struggle. He was to be 'Adam's son' sharing 'Adam's doom' and 'drain throughout life a mixed and moderate cup of enjoyment'.

The result is a plain tale, generally credible in its incidents, lacking romantic improbabilities or dramatic events.

'My narrative,' writes William Crimsworth, the hero, 'is not exciting . . . it may interest some individuals, who, having toiled in the same vocation as myself, will find in my experience frequent reflections of their own.' The vocation referred to is teaching, and the novel celebrates the teaching life. 'Professor', as

Charlotte Brontë carefully points out to us, in Belgium means not the head of a university department, but simply 'teacher'. But the most significant theme in the novel is the working out of Adam's doom, teaching being simply the area of activity in which the moral and economic concerns of the novel can be demonstrated.

There is not much to be said in favour of the novel, which suffers from the limitations imposed upon the author's imagination, but it is interesting in terms of her later development as a writer.

William Crimsworth is the typical Charlotte Brontë protagonist in that he is an orphan and penniless. Being without love, money, or worldly position, he is at once under the necessity of finding affection and earning a living. And this necessity Charlotte generally views as involving moral danger. Typically also, Crimsworth has the required qualities of independence and moral principle to bring him safely through.

ADAM'S DOOM—ECONOMICS AND MORALS

Economics, in the sense of earning a living, dominate Crimsworth's life. He must earn a salary. But complicating this is the need to find work which will allow him not only to be independent, but also to be uncorrupted.

The search for such an occupation involves him in a series of situations, each calculated to test his ideals. He rejects the help of his uncles because he will not suffer patronage, especially the patronage of those who ill-treated his mother. He leaves his brother's employ because he will not tolerate slavery and his brother's tyranny. 'I have now,' he tells Edward Crimsworth, 'given your service three months' trial, and I find it the most nauseous slavery.' Giving up his job as a clerk leaves him without hope of further support, but he had escaped 'without injury' to his 'self-respect'.

Armed with a letter of introduction, he leaves England for Belgium, and finds a teaching post in a boys' school owned by Monsieur Pelet, and later is invited to do part-time teaching at Mademoiselle Zoraïde Reuter's Pensionnat de Demoiselles.

He resigns his post at the Pensionnat on the grounds that Mademoiselle Reuter is a hypocrite, deceiving him particularly over one of the teachers at the school, Mademoiselle Henri, with whom he is in love. Mademoiselle Reuter has unjustly dismissed her. Although it will mean that he is once more penniless, he next gives up his post with Pelet because, since Pelet is about to marry Mademoiselle Reuter, who has already made some advances to Crimsworth, he sees the probability that 'in three months' time, a practical modern French novel would be in full process of concoction under the roof of the unsuspecting Pelet'.

Crimsworth is fortunate, however, in obtaining, a little later, an appointment as English professor at another College with a salary of three thousand francs per annum.

The motivation for Crimsworth's actions is, therefore, strongly moral, but despite this, the economic, seen in terms of pounds, shillings and pence, is dominant:

'Looking steadily to the needful! How can I do otherwise? I must live, and to live I must have what you call the "needful", which I can only get by working,' Crimsworth says to his friend Yorke Hunsden. Giving up his position with Mademoiselle Reuter on moral grounds, he reflects, 'I had voluntarily cut off £20 from my yearly income; I had diminished my £60 per annum to £40'; and after leaving M. Pelet's establishment: 'Had I retained my £60 per annum I could, now that Frances was in possession of £50, have gone straight to her this very evening...' His moral reflections make Crimsworth appear a prig, and his economic calculations tend to take the place of genuine emotional reaction to life.

LOVE AND MARRIAGE

The second aspect of Adam's doom is the experience of love, and the making of a satisfactory marriage. This is a concern of each of Charlotte Brontë's novels, and she sees it again as involving moral insight and choice. She had strong beliefs about the necessary conditions for the ideal marriage, and these concerned the right character on the part of the husband and wife and the establishing of the right balance in their relationship.

Charlotte once wrote in a letter:

> I was amused by what she [a friend] says respecting her wish that, when she marries, her husband will, at least, have a will of his own, even should he be a tyrant. Tell her, when she forms that aspiration again, she must make it conditional: if her husband has a strong will, he must also have strong sense, a kind heart, and a thoroughly correct notion of justice; because a man with a *weak brain* and a *strong will* is merely an intractable brute . . . A *tyrant* under any circumstances is a curse.   MRS. GASKELL, Chapter XVI

Charlotte admired men who were strong in will. She expected in marriage to be 'well-ruled and ordered' by an 'exacting, rigid, law-giving, passionate husband'. But this did not imply slave-like submission to an ignorant tyranny, and as she wrote to Ellen Nussey: 'I could not sit all day long making a grave face before my husband. I would laugh, and satirise, and say whatever came into my head first. And if he were a clever man, and loved me, the whole world, weighed in the balance against his smallest wish, should be light as air.' (Mrs. Gaskell, Chapter VIII)

In *The Professor*, Crimsworth's character is well-established, within the limitations of the novel, as coming up to these standards. He has will, sense, a kind heart, a correct notion of justice. He is exacting, law-giving and passionate. But he must also develop an insight and understanding of the female character in order to choose a wife wisely, and thus there is established in the novel the notion of the feminine ideal.

Many women are rejected by him—his brother's wife on the grounds of her lack of intelligence, the students at the girls' school because of the viciousness inherent in their natures: '. . . they had all been carefully brought up, yet was the mass of them depraved.' Mademoiselle Reuter is rejected because she 'consulted jealousy as an adviser, and employed treachery as an instrument'.

The first approval of a woman comes in the discussion between Yorke Hunsden and Crimsworth about Crimsworth's mother's picture:

> 'That is a good picture,' he continued, recurring to the portrait. 'Do you consider the face pretty?' I asked.

'Pretty! no—how can it be pretty, with sunk eyes and hollow cheeks? but it is peculiar; it seems to think. You could have a talk with that woman, if she were alive, on other subjects than dress, visiting, and compliments.'   Chapter III

Thus thoughtfulness and intelligence in a woman take precedence over beauty, and Frances Evans Henri, the teacher at Mademoiselle Reuter's school, has these qualities.

TYPICAL CHARLOTTE HEROINE—A FIRST SKETCH

In this novel we have a *description* (not a successful presentation) of Charlotte's ideal of womanhood. Mademoiselle Henri has many of the passive qualities of the Victorian heroine. She is the 'personification of discretion and forethought, of diligence and perseverance, of self-denial and self-control'. Taken in one dose, these accumulated virtues are difficult to swallow. But she has also the necessary qualities of independence, truth and honour, and 'the flame of natural passion burning under the eye of reason'. Frances Evans Henri is the first sketch of the typical Charlotte-heroine, in her typical posture—orphaned, little, plain, unnoticed, poor, but independent of spirit, firm of principle, and ambitious. Had Charlotte chosen to present the story through her eyes, the novel might have been less wooden. As it is, we see her only through Crimsworth's eyes, and in this way the main characteristic of her heroine is smothered—her strong, spirited egoism, which is revealed through thought and feeling as much as through deed.

Even in agreeing to marry Crimsworth, Frances insists on being allowed to continue her profession. She must be no encumbrance to him, no burden in any way. But more significantly:

Think of my marrying you to be kept by you, monsieur! I could not do it; and how dull my days would be . . . I should get depressed and sullen, and you would soon tire of me . . . I must act in some way, and act with you. I have taken notice, monsieur, that people who are only in each other's company for amusement, never really like each other so well, or esteem each other so highly, as those who work together, and perhaps suffer together.   Chapter XXIII

So Jane Eyre wishes to continue as Adèle's governess after her marriage, and reflects that if she had a 'small independency' Rochester would not be tempted to look upon her as a mistress.

What is desired, therefore, is not simply economic independence. It is the circumstances in which a woman can feel that she is an individual in her own right, has her own worth and interests, and this results in a kind of equality in work and feeling which leads to mutual esteem between husband and wife. 'Monsieur,' Frances tells Crimsworth, 'if a wife's nature loathes that of the man she is wedded to, marriage must be slavery. Against slavery all right thinkers revolt.'

To present such a relationship successfully within the pages of a novel is beyond Charlotte Brontë's powers at this stage, but however much we may regret her attempt, the ideal of mutual intercourse on all levels is what she strives to show. Thus, Frances Henri is, at the same time, 'Madame the directress, a stately and elegant woman', and Crimsworth's 'own little lace-mender'. It is 'her pleasure, her joy to make him (still) the master in all things'.

THE MASTER–PUPIL RELATIONSHIP

Such a relationship requires a degree of knowledge about each other on the part of husband and wife, and such knowledge can only be gained by observing each other in close contact in various situations. In *The Professor* it is the master–pupil relationship that gives opportunity for acquiring this knowledge.

This relationship, springing from Charlotte's own experiences as teacher and pupil, appears in each of her novels. At its most interesting, it takes the form of female pupil, male master. The activity involved is learning—generally of a language (Hindustani with Jane Eyre and St. John; French with Lucy Snowe and M. Paul; English with Frances and Crimsworth). But through the teaching and learning process comes a fuller understanding of character between master and pupil.

In *The Professor*, therefore, we have foreshadowed many of the themes which are to reappear in her later novels. There is the type of hero and heroine, the establishment of an ideal relation-

ship between them, a concern with moral and spiritual independence and integrity in the face of poverty and lack of love, the
recognition of the rightness of ambition, even in a female, and a
general distrust of physical beauty.

REASONS FOR THE NOVEL'S FAILURE

But *The Professor* was rejected because it was a bad novel, and it
was a bad novel for several reasons. In the first place, it is the
work of a writer who is yet unskilled in certain technical matters
such as plotting and character development. In the second place,
in dealing with what she thought was 'real', Charlotte was in
effect dealing with what were economic concerns. Thus the
concern with earning a living and achieving economic independence tends to take the place of the pressures of suffering,
aspiration, passion. In the third place, Charlotte was unfair to
herself in imposing unnatural limits on her genius by cutting
herself off entirely from the romantic imagination.

The structure of the novel is imperfect and irritating. We begin
with a quite uncalled-for letter from Crimsworth to an old school
friend telling him how, after he left Eton, he turned to his brother
for help. The letter was 'sent a year since', and the copy is now
found by Crimsworth accidentally. 'To this letter I never got an
answer,' he records, but 'The leisure time I have at command, and
which I intended to employ for his private benefit, I shall now
dedicate to that of the public at large . . . The above letter will
serve as an introduction. I now proceed.' As the first chapter of a
novel, this is extraordinarily maladroit. It lacks integration with
the rest of the novel, there is no sense of anything dynamic in
subject or style, indeed the reader is almost discouraged from
proceeding.

Within the general pattern, the emphases fall haphazard. There
is rarely a sense of building up to a significant scene, rarely a
sense of conflict of any kind where there is any doubt as to the
outcome, rarely a sense of true personalities in contact.

The story is told as a first person narrative by the hero,
William Crimsworth. First person narrative was to prove to be
Charlotte Brontë's strength in *Jane Eyre*, but she makes the

mistake here of having a male instead of a female narrator. Her attempt to portray a man's mentality and a man's world is unsuccessful. Primarily, between man and man, she adopts a brusque, abrupt method of communication which rarely varies, and which reflects back on all the male characters in a kind of limited harshness:

'Confound it! How doggedly self-approving the lad looks! I thought he was fit to die with shame, and there he sits grinning smiles . . .'

'Hunsden—you spoke of grapes; I was thinking of a fruit I like better . . . It is of no use your offering me the draught of bitterness . . . I have the anticipation of sweetness on my palate; the hope of freshness on my lips; I can reject the unsavoury, and endure the exhausting.'

'For how long?'

'Till the next opportunity for effort; and as the prize of success will be a treasure after my own heart, I'll bring a bull's strength to the struggle.'

'Bad luck crushes bulls as easily as bullaces . . . you were born with a wooden spoon in your mouth, depend on it.'

'I believe you . . . grasped firmly, and handled nimbly, even a wooden spoon will shovel up broth.' Chapter XXII

The use of oaths—'Confound it'; of abrupt phrases and rhetorical questions; of crude images—'shovel up broth'; of colloquial terms—'lad', represents Charlotte's attempt to render male conversation, when no ladies are present. That she found it a strain is indicated, I think, by the amount of conversation that is carried on in terms of fairly far-fetched imagery, and the lack of real bite beneath. The struggle between Hunsden and Crimsworth, after the former has met Frances, is reminiscent of the behaviour of two schoolboys and has an uncomfortable and contrived air:

No sooner had we got into the street than Hunsden collared me.

'And that is your lace-mender?' he said; '. . . You, scion of Seacombe, have proved your disdain of social distinctions by taking up with an *ouvrière*! And I pitied the fellow . . .'

'Just let go my collar, Hunsden.'

On the contrary, he swayed me to and fro; so I grappled him

round the waist. It was dark; the street lonely and lampless. We had then a tug for it; and after we had both rolled on the pavement, and with difficulty picked ourselves up, we agreed to walk on more soberly.
Chapter XXIV

But the inept dialogue extends throughout the book, and some of the love scenes are particularly painful to read as a result.

Crimsworth's smugness and self-sufficiency must be apparent from the quotations already given. He does not develop through vicissitude or fortune. He is given to such reflections as: 'There you cannot dream, you cannot speculate and theorise—there you shall out and work!'; '. . . at least, ere I deviate, I will advance far enough to see whither my career tends'; '. . . the idea of marrying a doll or a fool was always abhorrent to me.'

STYLISTIC FAULTS

As a result of the slackness of narrative, certain stylistic habits of Charlotte Brontë's—irritating at any time—now stand out in an uncomfortable relief. There is her habit of addressing the reader, for example. I have quoted one example of this. There are many others. Invariably, they come at a time of lessened emotional interest, draw attention to themselves, and break the sense of a fictional world. Often they reveal themselves as a half-disguised form of Charlotte thinking about her narrative technique. After Crimsworth's meeting with M. Pelet, we have: 'Well, and what was he like? and what were my impressions concerning him?' After his introduction to Mlle. Reuter and the Pensionnat de Demoiselles, 'What had I known of female character previously to my arrival at Brussels? Precious little.' And on the same subject: 'Know, O incredulous reader! that a master stands in a somewhat different relation towards a pretty, light-headed, probably ignorant girl . . .'

Charlotte Brontë's habit of presenting mental or emotional conflict in character by means of personification—a stilted proceeding at any time—here stands out embarrassingly given the lack of emotional conviction behind it: '. . . all at once out spoke Conscience—"Down, stupid tormentors!" cried she; "the man

49

has done his duty; you shall not bait him thus . . ." ' At times, the use of personification becomes comic: 'When I left Ostend on a mild February morning, and found myself on the road to Brussels, nothing could look vapid for me . . . Liberty I clasped in my arms for the first time, and the influence of her smile and embrace revived my life like the sun and the west wind.'

Charlotte's experiment at taking 'truth and nature' for her guides may not have been successful, but the working over her Brussels experience in a realistic form was to prove a useful exercise when she came to write *Villette*.

4

Jane Eyre

'. . . imagination is a strong, restless faculty, which claims to be heard and exercised: are we to be quite deaf to her cry, and insensate to her struggles? When she shows us bright pictures, are we never to look at them, and try to reproduce them?' So Charlotte Brontë wrote to G. H. Lewes when, after the publication of *Jane Eyre*, he advised her not to stray too far from the ground of experience. Certainly, in *Jane Eyre*, she had moved from the prosaic and ordinary world of *The Professor* into the realms of imagination and romance.

The immediate popularity of the novel is shown by the sales— within five months of publication, three editions were published. And if we consider the novel simply as a story, its fascination at the circulating library level is clear. The pathetic tale of an orphan, abused by her aunt and guardian, sent to a harsh charity school where conditions bring about an epidemic of fever and her friend dies, must arouse answering sympathy in the reader. That the same girl should, at the age of eighteen, become governess to an illegitimate child in a large house whose master falls in love with and tries to inveigle her into a bigamous marriage, even though his mad wife is imprisoned in the house, must hold the reader at least on the level of excitement. That the heroine should, with great suffering, tear herself away from this situation to suffer want and obscurity, find herself to be an heiress, reject another proposal of marriage and seek out her former master and marry, satisfies all our feelings that such virtue should be rewarded.

The source material that went into the making of the novel is very mixed. From Charlotte's own experience, there is obviously the period at the Clergy Daughters' School, and the life at Haworth Parsonage, as well as her teaching days. But much of what makes up the novel is conventional in the fictional sense. There are well-established literary sources which demand a specific and strong response from the reader.

Jane is a Cinderella figure to begin with, without the beauty of a Cinderella, but with all the sympathy such a figure draws through being pushed aside, ill-treated and ignored. And her story, with its gradual recognition of her virtues and strengths, is the romantic tale of Cinderella who marries her prince. But it is also, in part, the story of Pamela (of whom Jane is told by Bessie), the servant girl of Richardson's novel who resists her master's attempts to seduce her and eventually becomes his wife. This basis in romantic folk-tale and the novel of seduction gives the story a great deal of its fascination.

On one level we have all the trappings—in the central section especially—of the Gothic horror novel. There is the 'demoniac laugh—low, suppressed, and deep—uttered, as it seemed, at the very keyhole of [her] chamber door'; the mysterious apartment on the third floor; Mason with one arm 'almost soaked in blood', with a 'corpse-like face'; the mad woman who 'grovelled, seemingly, on all fours'.

In this situation Jane Eyre is as cool and courageous as any Gothic heroine. She puts out the fire in Rochester's bed, and sits alone with Mason in the night bathing his wounded arm.

In Rochester, there is something of Richardson's rakes—Mr. B. and Lovelace, and of the Gothic villain. But there is also something of the Byronic hero with his rough charm, mysterious background, his wild life, brusque, often cruel manner, but tragic and strong emotions.

All of these are, individually, good 'story-lines'. Brought together they make a powerful mixture. And there is no sense of their clashing since all draw upon the same fundamental emotional response and are united in the strong, passionate figure of Jane.

But this same novel, made up of such popular and traditional literary elements, was to call forth from some reviewers such accusations as: 'Pre-eminently an anti-Christian composition . . . a murmuring against . . . God's appointment' and 'an undue reliance on self, unamiable . . . if not positively irreligious'. This draws our attention to other, more serious tones in the novel, to concerns with more fundamental issues than those of the pathetic or Gothic tale.

THE QUESTION POSED

Serious questions about life and morals are constantly being posed in the midst of the romantic and Gothic situations. How is one to live within the situation in which God has placed one? How does one suffer tyranny, cruelty? How does one control strong emotion? How does one live in barren circumstances? How does one keep one's religious and moral integrity, while still satisfying the individual sense of justice and rightness? Does one rebel, as the young Jane does? accept with Christian meekness as Helen does? become a liar and hypocrite for the sake of a piece of gingerbread? control one's passions to obey God's precepts no matter what the personal cost?

This serious vein of philosophical inquiry about life is an important part of the novel. It is revealed for example in the pronouncements about the guiding principles of religion and morals which arise from a conversation or as a result of an incident. Thus Mr. Rochester, speaking of his determination to change his aim and motives in life, states that he will pass a law that both these are right:

> 'They cannot be, sir, if they require a new statute to legalise them.' [says Jane]
> 'They are, Miss Eyre, though they absolutely require a new statute: unheard-of combinations of circumstances demand unheard-of rules.'
> 'That sounds a dangerous maxim, sir; because one can see at once that it is liable to abuse . . . You are human and fallible . . . The human and fallible should not arrogate a power with which the divine and perfect alone can be safely entrusted.'
> 'What power?'
> 'That of saying of any strange, unsanctioned line of action, "Let it be right." '   Chapter 14

Such inquiry and such attempts to answer fundamental questions take place on the childish level with the young Jane:

> 'Do you know where the wicked go after death?'
> 'They go to hell,' was my ready and orthodox answer.
> 'And what is hell? Can you tell me that?'
> 'A pit full of fire.'
> 'And should you like to fall into that pit, and to be burning there for ever?'
> 'No, sir.'
> 'What must you do to avoid it?'
> I deliberated a moment: my answer, when it did come was objectionable: 'I must keep in good health, and not die.'

Again, a conversation with St. John involves a discussion of the types of philosopher:

> 'You would describe yourself as a mere pagan philosopher,' I said.
> 'No. There is this difference between me and deistic philosophers: I believe; and I believe the Gospel. You missed your epithet. I am not a pagan, but a Christian philosopher—a follower of the sect of Jesus. As His disciple I adopt His pure, His merciful, His benignant doctrines . . .'
>
> Chapter 32

Far from being an anti-Christian novel, therefore, *Jane Eyre* is concerned throughout with questions of moral and Christian behaviour, to an even greater extent than was *The Professor*. And while, in the first novel, God was a distant observer of his creatures, He becomes here an active participant in the action. The characters are much aware of God and His teachings, and interpret His will and doctrines in terms of their own fate and actions.

So we have Bessie's song of the orphan child, early in the novel, pointing to Jane's orphaned and lonely path in life:

> Ev'n should I fall o'er the broken bridge passing,
>   Or stray in the marshes, by false lights beguiled,
> Still will my Father, with promise and blessing,
>   Take to his bosom the poor orphan child.

And so Jane, having left Rochester, concludes: 'God must have led me on', and 'Sure was I of His efficiency to save what He had made.' And so St. John mistakenly concludes: 'God and nature intended you for a missionary's wife.' And so Rochester tells her, eventually, 'Of late, Jane—only—only of late—I began to see and acknowledge the hand of God in my doom.'

There is, also, a strong sense of God's justice at work *in this life* in terms of punishment and reward, rather than in an afterlife. Though Helen Burns looks to happiness in a future life, Rochester's maiming and blinding, Jane's wanderings and sufferings, and their ultimate reunion take place in this world.

Thus God, often working through accident or nature, is very much present in the world of the novel.

PATH OF THE HEROINE THROUGH LIFE

Jane Eyre's story, therefore, as well as being that of a romantic and Gothic heroine is also a progression in moral and spiritual terms. The situations in which she finds herself require that she should learn a Christian attitude to her own nature and to life, and she is tested in this learning. Her marriage to Rochester is not merely the conventionally romantic union of the novel, but a coming together of two sinners who have repented and suffered and whose union is thus sanctioned by God.

Choice in this novel is no longer a matter of leaving a job on moral grounds, but of obeying the precepts of God and religion —and of one's own nature—in the face of the direct consequences. Nor does Jane find a Christian attitude to life easy, as Crimsworth did. 'False lights' do beguile, and thus the smugness of the earlier novel is avoided.

The first part of *Jane Eyre* can be seen in terms of a learning process, the second in terms of putting the knowledge gained into practice.

Jane Eyre has certain strong characteristics. She is passionate and imaginative—human sympathies and affections have a powerful hold on her. She thinks 'too much of the love of human beings'. She longs for a wide experience of life. She is clear-sighted and candid; she cannot dissemble or be deceitful.

She begins with these natural propensities, but at first, being in a false situation and without knowledge or learning, she is wild and unhappy. She has pagan ideas of reacting to hurts— an eye for an eye and a tooth for a tooth: 'I will never call you aunt again as long as I live. I will never come to see you when I am grown up; and if any one asks me how I liked you, and how you treated me, I will say the very thought of you makes me sick, and that you treated me with miserable cruelty,' she tells Mrs. Reed. So she successfully routs her aunt, but she realises that such a doctrine of revenge does not make for happiness. Mrs. Reed leaves her in possession of the field, but unrestrained passion leads inevitably to the reaction: 'A child cannot quarrel with its elders . . . cannot give its furious feelings uncontrolled play . . . without experiencing afterwards the pang of remorse and the chill of reaction.' As a result of the treatment she receives and her reaction to it, she feels only bad emotions surging in her breast.

At Lowood, Helen Burns undergoes a greater cruelty and tyranny, but she tells Jane: 'It is not violence that best overcomes hate—nor vengeance that most certainly heals injury . . . Love your enemies; bless them that curse you; do good to them that hate you and despitefully use you.'

From Helen, Jane learns to bear shame without showing her suffering, she learns to control her hatred when telling Miss Temple her story, but she cannot share Helen's rejection of the world, or her logical view of a matter. When Helen points out that not everybody believes Jane a liar since only eighty have heard her called so, Jane objects, 'But what have I to do with millions! The eighty I know despise me.' And she goes on, ' . . . if others don't love me, I would rather die than live.'

It is from Miss Temple that Jane learns how to control her passionate nature: 'I had imbibed from her something of her nature and much of her habits; more harmonious thoughts; what seemed better regulated feelings . . . I appeared a disciplined and subdued character.'

Thus, when she leaves Lowood, she has learned to control her nature while retaining those aspects of it which are good; she has still the 'power to be tranquil' when there is a 'reason for tranquillity'. But her learning has not been tested. It is tested at Thornfield. On the grounds of her learning in moral and religious principle, Jane gives Rochester excellent theoretical advice: '. . . nothing free-born would submit to [insolence], even for a salary'; 'Repentance is said to be [remorse's] cure'.

In reply, Rochester calls her a 'neophyte, that have not passed the porch of life, and are absolutely unacquainted with its mysteries'.

IDOLATRY AND THE LAW GIVEN BY GOD

The world for her is to be Thornfield Hall, and her testing is to be in terms of that craving for love which she has always felt. She shows herself equal to the occasion. She can control her emotions even under Mr. Rochester's pretence of being in love with Blanche Ingram, but once his love for her is declared, she gives hers whole-heartedly: 'My future husband was becoming my whole world . . . almost my hope of heaven. He stood between me and every thought of religion, as an eclipse intervenes between man and the broad sun. I could not, in those days, see God for His creature: of whom I had made an idol.' She is falling into the sin of idolatry—the failing of her passionate nature.

After the broken marriage ceremony comes Jane's greatest testing. Is idolatry to win? If she leaves him, she is faced with immense suffering: a suffering increased by the knowledge of *his* suffering and the further degradation he might be led to. All that is required of her, to obtain their mutual happiness, is the transgression of 'a mere human law'. And Jane reflects, 'Who in the world cares for *you*? or who will be injured by what you do?' It is a mere matter of a convention to be broken.

But her answer takes her back to that principle she earlier enunciated to Rochester: 'The human and fallible should not arrogate a power with which the divine and perfect alone can be safely entrusted . . . That of saying of any strange, unsanctioned line of action "Let it be right." '

And she answers:

> '*I* care for myself. The more solitary . . . the more I will respect
> myself. I will keep the law given by God; sanctioned by man . . .
> Laws and principles are not for times when there is no temptation:
> they are for such moments as this, when body and soul rise in
> mutiny against their rigour . . .   Chapter 27

The action she takes—right though it may be to her—is most
difficult in that she 'had no solace from self-approbation; none
even from self-respect'.

RELIGION CALLS

With the Rivers family, Jane achieves something of the equilib-
rium of her years with Miss Temple. She has now a 'small independence', she has a home, and she has affection from the Rivers
sisters. Passion is controlled. Life is to be a sheltered and moderate
existence. But a further testing is due—this time in the other
direction. Passion must be given up altogether, independence,
life itself, in the dedication of her life to God's work as a missionary.

In trying to persuade her to this loveless existence, St. John is
as mistaken as to her nature as was Rochester, who tried to dress
her in jewels and silks and put her in the position of his former
mistresses: 'God and nature [says St. John] intended you for a
missionary's wife. It is not personal, but mental endowments
they have given you: you are formed for labour, not for love.'
For both Rochester and St. John, she is to be the 'instrument' of
good: 'But the instrument—the instrument! God, who does the
work, ordains the instrument. I have myself—I tell it you without
parable—been a worldly, dissipated, restless man; and I believe
I have found the instrument for my cure' [says Rochester].
And Jane objects to St. John's plan on the grounds that: 'He
prizes me as a soldier would a good weapon, and that is all . . .
such a martyrdom would be monstrous.'

Yet, under the pressures St. John puts upon her, she almost
yields: 'I was tempted to cease struggling with him—to rush
down the torrent of his will into the gulf of his existence, and
there lose my own. I was almost as hard beset by him now as I

had been once before, in a different way, by another [Rochester]. I was a fool both times. To have yielded then would have been an error of principle; to have yielded now would have been an error of judgment.' But 'Religion called—Angels beckoned—God commanded—life rolled together like a scroll—death's gates opening showed eternity beyond . . .' It is the vision and sacrifice of Helen Burns.

But the voice of Rochester calling to her, breaks the spell: 'Down superstition . . . This is not thy deception, nor thy witchcraft: it is the work of nature. She was roused, and did—no miracle—but her best.'

Rochester, maimed and blinded, but now acknowledging God's goodness, is a fit mate for Jane, who has also gone through the tempering fire of misery and temptation.

A PILGRIM'S PROGRESS

Thus the pathetic and Gothic story is the vehicle for demonstrating the working out of a Christian theme. Viewed in this way, *Jane Eyre* is an unusual novel, since it is a kind of pilgrim's progress presented in terms of the Gothic and romantic world and of passionate sexual love. It is an allegory in the sense that it is a moral and religious discourse under the guise of a popular novel.

But it is not a progress towards spirituality and the renunciation of this world. The two major temptations undergone by Jane are first towards the passionate and worldly in defiance of God's laws, and secondly towards the dedicated and spiritual in defiance of her own nature. Jane can accept neither. The allegory is a defence of the individual's right to seek his own way—worldly or other-worldly—provided he transgresses no divine law in doing this.

In her preface to the second edition, Charlotte Brontë made clear this concern of hers with a moral theme. She attacks those who have criticised the novel, those 'whose ears detect in each protest against bigotry—that parent of crime—an insult to piety, that regent of God on earth'. She then states 'certain simple truths':

Conventionality is not morality, self-righteousness is not religion. To attack the first is not to assail the last. To pluck the mask from the face of the Pharisee, is not to lift an impious hand to the Crown of Thorns . . . appearance should not be mistaken for truth; narrow human doctrines . . . should not be substituted for the world-redeeming creed of Christ.

Whatever intentions she may have had in writing the novel to create something 'wild, wonderful, and thrilling', this firmly moral and religious view could not be kept out.

STRUCTURE

It has been objected that Charlotte Brontë's novels are faulty in structure. Except in the case of *Shirley*, she follows a good portion of the life of an individual in a rather rambling, haphazard manner. There is no plot tightly-knit, carefully constructed round a central idea as there is in the novels of Jane Austen, nor is there the careful portioning of time to the stages of development in the protagonist's career, as we find in some of Hardy's novels. The novels are closer to the picaresque novel, such as *Tom Jones* and *Joseph Andrews*, where we are given a multiplicity of events and characters, loosely connected to the protagonist, and designed to present a wide range of human types. We cannot, however, justify Charlotte Brontë's structural method in these terms—her themes and setting limit the world she presents to the schoolroom and its immediate environs.

But the close reader of her novels must ask such questions as why, in *The Professor*, is space given to Yorke Hunsden who appears and disappears from the plot with little justification? Why should almost three pages of that novel in Chapter 25 be given over to a detailed description of the non-dramatic event of a walk in the countryside in order that Frances might ask permission to start a school of her own?

Similarly, in *Jane Eyre*, some detailed descriptions are given of Eliza and Georgiana Reed, which have little bearing on Jane's life, and do not forward the plot. And while Chapters 5 to 10 deal with Jane's life as pupil and teacher at Lowood Institute, four months—from January to May in the year of her arrival—are given in detail with emphasis upon the character and fate of Helen Burns—a character who plays no further part in the action. Moreover, the remaining five and a half years of Jane's stay at the school are passed over in half a chapter.

Such apparently haphazard selection of character and emphasis upon incident might be due to lack of skill on the part of an author, unless we can find justification for it in terms of the novel. In *The Professor* such justification is not easily found, and if found, carries little satisfaction. The case is rather different with *Jane Eyre*.

Many of the apparently unnecessary emphases in the novel can be seen to be related to the moral and religious themes. Jane's life can be seen in terms of a pilgrim's progress, but Jane's progress is towards the finding of a satisfactory reconciliation between her desires and passions and the moral and religious convictions, but it is a reconciliation which must take place in the present life, and not in terms of a future life, or through a renunciation of worldly pleasures and ambitions. Thus, emphasis upon an incident, or upon a character, may be linked to this theme.

CHARACTERS AS TYPES OF VIRTUES AND VICES

Helen Burns must be developed fully to bring out an example of suffering which is met with a Christian forbearance and forgiveness that Jane can never emulate, because Helen is attuned to the life hereafter, not to this world. 'By dying young,' she tells Jane, 'I shall escape great sufferings. I had not qualities or talents to make my way very well in the world: I should have been continually at fault.' Thus, Helen can wear 'patient and unresentful' Miss Scatcherd's pasteboard with the word 'slattern' written on it, round her forehead. But Jane must tear it off: 'The fury of which she was incapable had been burning in my soul all day.' And Jane, cleared of the bad character Mr. Brocklehurst had given her, can settle happily to preparing herself for the future by getting herself an education. Thought of eternal life makes Lowood bearable to Helen, but Jane, filled with thoughts of learning drawing and French, 'would not now have exchanged

Lowood with all its privations for Gateshead and its daily luxuries'.

Similarly, St. John's love for Rosamund Oliver is given some prominence in Jane's story. We may conclude that it does, at least, give further insight into St. John's character, but it is more intimately connected with the serious themes of the novel, and provides a parallel example of a strong sexual passion to stand beside Jane's love for Rochester. Jane has left Rochester, has controlled her passion, on moral grounds, but her love for him remains. But St. John rejects love as 'a mere fever of the flesh'. As did Helen Burns, he has turned from all worldly things, but because religion has developed his natural characteristics of rationality and personal ambition into tools for the service of Christ. Again, Jane is set against a character faced with similar worldly problems to herself, who rejects the world for the spiritual.

This opposition in their attitude to what are the 'good' things of life for them, is shown when Jane, happy in her legacy and newly-discovered relatives—the consolations of this world for her—proposes preparing Moor House for her cousin's return:

> 'It is all very well for the present,' said he, 'but seriously, I trust when the first flush of vivacity is over, you will look a little higher than domestic endearments and household joys.'
> 'The best thing the world has!' I interrupted.

The two Reed sisters can be justified in the novel on the same terms. Their appearance in some detail, though without forwarding the action of the plot, shows them as types of human beings set in contrast to Jane and her problems. Georgiana is the type of worldly selfishness and vanity, Eliza is the type of spiritual selfishness and vanity. They are 'two natures rendered, the one intolerably acrid, the other despicably savourless' for the want of generous feeling.

CHARACTER PRESENTATION—THE SIGNIFICANCE OF APPEARANCE

Characters, therefore, are grouped, as in *The Professor*, in relation to theme. In *The Professor*, dissimulation being one of the main faults that are condemned, M. Pelet and Mademoiselle Reuter, with their respective mothers, are arranged on the side of deviousness and in opposition to the candour, honesty, and outspokenness of Crimsworth, Frances, and Yorke Hunsden. And Jane's progress through life brings her into contact with many types of nature whose leanings are either towards the spiritual or towards the worldly.

The function of the character in the novel is thus determined by the fundamentally moral approach, and Charlotte's method of drawing character is of the same kind.

Generally, physical appearance is of great importance because, in her novels, physical characteristics give the clue to character. St. John's face comes near to 'the antique models', his lineaments are 'harmonious', but 'there was something about his nostril, his mouth, his brow, which . . . indicated elements within either restless, or hard, or eager'.

Some characters' appearances reveal immediately the nature of the person, their physical characteristics frequently referring back symbolically to personality traits. Yorke Hunsden in *The Professor*, has 'small, and even feminine' lineaments, but these contrast strongly with his tall figure and the impression he gives in his voice and bearing 'of something powerful and massive'. This contrast suggests conflict 'between his inward and outward man . . . his soul had more of will than his body had of fibre and muscle . . . the athletic mind scowled scorn on its more fragile companion'.

This tendency to point to those physical characteristics which indicate character traits also at times takes the form of using terms from the sciences of physiognomy (the interpreting of the signs of the face) and phrenology (the interpreting of the signs of the skull). These pseudo-sciences were popular in Charlotte Brontë's day, and she herself consulted, under an assumed name, a phrenologist who found in her 'very remarkable' intellectual power and 'a fine organ of language'.

Such presentation of outward signs that point to inward characteristics determine nature and character for the reader and for other characters in the novels. Physiognomy and phrenology also foster the idea of variety within individual character—a conception which, in a novel, helps to avoid the static and oversimplified view of character. Thus, William Crimsworth's intention to be a tradesman is mocked at by Yorke Hunsden, on the evidence of his 'bumps of ideality, comparison, self-esteem, conscientiousness'. Rochester has well-developed intellectual organs, no signs of benevolence, but he does have a conscience.

Appearance is rarely deceptive for even if there are contradictory aspects in an appearance, they can be read and interpreted. Thus, in *Villette*, Madame Beck first appears as 'a motherly, dumpy, little woman, in a large shawl, a wrapping-gown, and a clean, trim night-cap . . . Her complexion was fresh and sanguine, not too rubicund; her eye, blue and serene'. But there are contradictory signs also—'. . . her face offered contrast, too . . . their [her features'] outline was stern: her forehead was high but narrow; it expressed capacity and some benevolence, but no expanse . . . Her mouth was hard, it could be a little grim' (Chapter 8).

Generally then, the external characteristics are an unfailing key to the internal ones, and this extends even to dress. Both Lucy Snowe and Jane develop more beauty with love, and their dress lightens from things dark and Quaker-like to lighter and thinner materials as their natures expand. Frances Henri also becomes prettier with happiness and love.

Finally, however, it is a view of character fixed firmly in moral principle. It is benevolence, conscientiousness, sensibility which are expressed by these means as well as intelligence or capacity.

The most extended and significant use of such an approach to character is seen in Rochester's reading, as a gipsy woman, of Jane's features, the whole interpretation of her character being seen by him in relation to his plans to marry her, in spite of his mad wife: '. . . the eye . . . looks soft and full of feeling . . . it is susceptible . . . its pride and reserve only confirm me in my opinion. The eye is favourable . . . As to the mouth, it delights at times in laughter . . . mobile and flexible . . . it is a mouth which should speak much and smile often, and have human affection for its interlocutor. That feature too is propitious. I see no enemy to a fortunate issue but in the brow . . . The forehead declares, "Reason sits firm and holds the reins . . ." ' (Chapter 19).

It follows from this view of character, that St. John must be attracted by, and determinedly repulse, Rosamund Oliver. Rosamund appeals, in her perfection of beauty, entirely to the senses, and St. John's ascetic nature rejects inevitably such an appeal, even though he is so strongly aware of it:

> No charm was wanting, no defect was perceptible; the young girl had regular and delicate lineaments; eyes shaped and coloured as we see them in lovely pictures, large, and dark, and full; the long shadowy eyelash which encircles a fine eye with so soft a fascination; the pencilled brow which gives such clearness; the white, smooth forehead . . . the cheek, oval, fresh, and smooth . . . Nature had surely formed her in a partial mood . . .   Chapter 31

Rosamund, in keeping with the method of character presentation in the novel, is at once a person and a symbol of all the worldly and sensuous and beautiful aspects of life which St. John's nature and ambition rejects. And, in keeping with Charlotte Brontë's general view of female character, being beautiful, she is yet deficient in character: 'She was coquettish, but not heartless; exacting, but not worthlessly selfish . . . hasty, but good-humoured; vain . . . but not affected . . . sufficiently intelligent, gay, lively, and unthinking . . . but she was not profoundly interesting or thoroughly impressive.'

PHYSICAL SETTING

A great deal of the power of the novel comes from the fact that each stage of Jane's journey is marked by an appropriate physical setting, a setting realised vividly and concretely by Jane.

There is the ability to conjure up, without the use of over-emotional language, the cold and hunger experienced by the girls at Lowood: the older girls standing before the fire and 'the younger children crouched [behind them] in groups, wrapping their starved arms in their pinafores'; 'the torture of thrusting the swelled, raw, and stiff toes into my shoes in the morning'; 'the secret tears' which result from half her food being taken by bigger girls.

The child's ability to find consolation in the midst of unhappiness, as Jane does, ensconced in the window seat at Gateshead Hall, warm and safe, but viewing the stormy world outside, lost in pictures her imagination draws up, is another aspect of this created reality. And a further side of it is her descriptions of nature which enhance the reality of a world in which so much that is incredible takes place: 'the little brown birds, which stirred occasionally in the hedge, looked like single russet leaves that had forgotten to drop'. But setting also takes on symbolical significance referring back to the moral and religious themes.

Charlotte Brontë's picture of society, for example, may be unreal and unconvincing at one level, but symbolically it is appropriate and appropriately presented. It is a shallow, glittering, empty, unpleasant world compared with the reality of her relationship with Rochester.

In a way that is close to an allegorical presentation of society, Thornfield becomes the rich, worldly setting with its carpets, hangings, plate, flowers, and bustling kitchen; the world enters with horses, veils, plumes—a cavalcade sweeping up the drive. The company presents a dazzling, superficial brilliance. The ladies descend the staircase 'as noiselessly as a bright mist rolls down a hill'; the dining-room is filled with light and lustre; the ladies have 'a sweeping amplitude of array that seemed to magnify their person as a mist magnifies the moon'.

But after these first impressions of worldly brilliancy, Jane Eyre sets to work on the reality beneath—the satirical laugh, the hard eye, the haughtiness. We are shown the superficiality of conversation, the idleness of mind, the dulness that steals over their spirits in the absence of diversions; the monetary motives; the insensitivity to effect in Blanche Ingram's denouncing of governesses in Mr. Rochester's presence with all it reveals of her character:

The Ladies Lynn and Ingram continued to consort in solemn con-
ferences, where they nodded their two turbans at each other, and
held up their four hands in confronting gestures of surprise or
mystery, or horror, . . . like a pair of magnified puppets. Mild Mrs.
Dent talked with good-natured Mrs. Eshton . . . Sir George Lynn,
Colonel Dent, and Mr. Eshton discussed politics, or county affairs,
or justice business. Lord Ingram flirted with Amy Eshton; Louisa
played and sang to and with one of the Messrs. Lynn; and Mary
Ingram listened languidly to the gallant speeches of the other.

Chapter 18

Against this almost allegorical picture of society, Rochester
stands out as a live, passionate, sympathetic human being: 'I
compared him with his guests . . . contrasted [them] with his
look of native pith and genuine power . . . I saw Mr. Rochester
smile—his stern features softened; his eye grew both brilliant
and gentle, its ray both searching and sweet . . .'

By a similar method, the orchard at Thornfield, at the time of
Rochester's proposal, gathers together the idea of the coming to
fruition of their love, the conception of a Garden of Eden, and at
the same time the symbolic threat to their happiness in Rochester's secret. 'Nature' in the two senses of the natural world and
man's innate disposition, is an important concern in the book,
and Jane is always in sympathy with the first, and concerned to
discover the second:

A splendid Midsummer shone over England . . . I went apart into
the orchard. No nook in the grounds more sheltered and more
Eden-like . . . a winding walk, bordered with laurels and terminating
in a giant horse-chestnut . . . led down to the fence . . . Sweet-brier
and southernwood, jasmine, pink, and rose have long been yielding
their evening sacrifice of incense; this new scent is neither of shrub
nor flower; it is . . . Mr. Rochester's cigar . . . I see trees laden with
fruit. I hear a nightingale . . .

And having made his proposal and been accepted, Rochester
defies man's opinion, and claims God's support in what he is
doing: 'It will expiate at God's tribunal. I know my Maker
sanctions what I do. For the world's judgment I wash my hands
thereof.' Immediately, nature sounds its warning: 'But what had

befallen the night? . . . we were all in shadow . . . And what ailed the chestnut tree? it writhed and groaned; while wind . . . came sweeping over us.' The storm breaks, and next morning 'the great horse-chestnut at the bottom of the orchard had been struck by lightning in the night, and half of it split away'.

This is the Gothic, romantic, natural, religious and symbolic world of the novel.

CHARACTER OF JANE

The strength of the novel lies in the figure of Jane who unites both the religious and moral themes and the romantic and Gothic ones. The greatest weakness of *The Professor* was its central character. The greatest strength of this novel is Jane.

According to Mrs. Gaskell, Charlotte Brontë

> once told her sisters that they were wrong—even morally wrong—in making their heroines beautiful as a matter of course. They replied that it was impossible to make a heroine interesting on any other terms. Her answer was, 'I will prove to you that you are wrong; I will show you a heroine as plain and as small as myself, who shall be as interesting as any of yours.' Hence Jane Eyre . . .
>
> MRS. GASKELL, Chapter XV

Jane was not, however, such a departure as Charlotte suggests, for she is, in fact, a development of Frances Evans Henri, being poor, plain, obscure like her.

Jane Eyre is not portrayed in any great psychological depth or subtlety. We never feel that she will make the wrong choice from deeply-held convictions as does Dorothea Brooke or Emma Woodhouse. But her character is strongly and appropriately developed within the limits of its range, and we are aware throughout the novel of the individual voice of Jane. Her character depends upon contrasts—small, plain and obscure as she is, she is passionate, courageous, and determinedly independent. It is this character, with its emphasis upon its right as an individual before God, which is heard in the novel from the beginning.

'Master! How is he my master? Am I a servant?' she demands

68

of Miss Abbot; 'Deceit is not my fault!' she exclaims to her aunt; 'I don't think, sir, you have the right to command me, merely because you are older than I or because you have seen more of the world than I have; your claim to superiority depends on the use you have made of your time and experience,' she tells Mr. Rochester.

OBJECTIONS TO THE NOVEL

But while one may be aware of Charlotte Brontë's aim and purpose in the book, may appreciate its varied elements held in suspension, may contemplate the use of the allegorical method, one may still have objections to the novel. One might say, for example, that the mad wife was an unnecessary and Gothic intrusion. Rochester might have been prevented from marrying Jane and have been plunged into a life of dissoluteness, by having a wife who had deserted or betrayed him.

One may feel irritated by the unshaken virtue of Jane, by her inverted vanity—poor and obscure, and small and plain as she is:

> 'If he expects me to talk for the mere sake of talking and showing off, he will find he has addressed himself to the wrong person.'

> . . . obliged to be plain—for I had no article of attire that was not made with extreme simplicity—I was still by nature solicitous to be neat . . . I ever wished to look as well as I could, and to please as much as my want of beauty would permit . . .

> Whether is it better, I ask, to be a slave in a fool's paradise at Marseilles . . . or to be a village school-mistress, free and honest, in a breezy mountain nook in the healthy heart of England?

One may object to the wild coincidences by which the plot is made to adhere—the discovery that Jane *is* an heiress, that the Rivers *are* her cousins.

One may feel that too much fuss is made over Jane and her moral predicament with Rochester; that moral and religious machinery of such weight should not be brought to the working out of an individual problem involving an attempt at bigamous marriage. Admitting the belief in a personal religion, and the individual's right to appeal to God, and the doctrine of the fall of the sparrow, can we nevertheless accept divine intervention through nature to bring the contrite Rochester his Jane and to save her from toiling under eastern suns and in Asian deserts as 'a conductress of Indian schools, and a helper amongst Indian women' in a climate in which she could not live long? Can we view Rochester's attempt to marry her as an attempt to sully an innocent flower which the 'Omnipotent snatched from [him]', afterwards forcing him through the shadow of death in punishment?

Finally one might object that having set out the predicament of her heroine in terms of a moral and religious conflict which leads her to leave her lover and endure much suffering in order to act according to her conscience, Charlotte then evades the whole issue by getting rid of the mad wife and all the other obstacles by sensational or miraculous means. She employed a sleight of hand in order to attain a happy conclusion, working out a serious moral and religious theme in terms of Gothic melodrama and romantic coincidence.

5

Shirley

At first glance, *Shirley* appears to have no relationship to Charlotte Brontë's other novels: it seems to be an attempt at another genre, an experiment she did not repeat. Although she was to tell Mr. Smith: 'I cannot write books handling the topics of the day; it is of no use trying. Nor can I write a book for its moral. Nor can I take up a philanthropic scheme', *Shirley* is, nevertheless, a departure in this direction, being a historical, social, provincial novel.

She returned for her subject to her memories of Miss Wooler's stories when she was at Roe Head—stories about the Luddite risings. She sent for files of the *Leeds Mercury* for the years 1812–1814, and she set the date of her novel on page two: 'but in eighteen-hundred-eleven-twelve that affluent rain [of curates] had not descended'.

The action of the novel is confined to the period from mid-February 1811 to June 1812, and the event which made these dates significant was the 'Orders in Council' forbidding trade with France which had offended America and cut off the principal markets of the Yorkshire wool trade:

> The 'Orders in Council' provoked by Napoleon's Milan and Berlin decrees, and forbidding neutral powers to trade with France, had, by offending America, cut off the principal market of the Yorkshire woollen trade, and brought it consequently to the verge of ruin . . . At this crisis, certain inventions in machinery were introduced into the staple manufactures of the north, which, greatly reducing the number of hands necessary to be employed, threw thousands out of work . . . A bad harvest supervened . . .
>
> SHIRLEY, Chapter II

The novel ends with the repeal of the Orders in Council: 'On the 18th of June 1812, the Orders in Council were repealed and the blockaded ports thrown open.'

She sets her novel in the north of England, specifically narrowing the setting to *one* area: 'A yell followed this demonstration—a rioters' yell—a North-of-England—a Yorkshire—a West-Riding—a West-Riding-clothing-district-of-Yorkshire rioters' yell.' In fact, the neighbourhood is that of Roe Head school which was situated 'on the right of the road from Leeds to Huddersfield'.

Mrs. Gaskell describes the area as one in which the woollen mills 'encroach upon and shoulder out the proprietors of the ancient halls'. Shirley's home of Fieldhead was based upon Oakwell Hall, a gentleman's residence that was but a mile from the woollen mills. Close to Roe Head was Rawfolds, a factory belonging to a Mr. Cartwright (a man with foreign blood in him who spoke French well), who employed machinery for dressing woollen cloth, and who, on 11 April 1812, defended his factory against a crowd of starving cloth-dressers. A fortnight later, another factory owner was shot dead on Crossland Moor.

Two miles from Roe Head lived Mr. Roberson, of Heald's Hall, vicar of Heckmondwike, an old-fashioned Tory, stern, fierce, and soldierly, who built, at his own cost, a fine church at Liversedge, and who had been a friend of Mr. Brontë during the latter's curacy at Hartshead.

Using the West Riding setting, Charlotte Brontë takes the parish of Briarhead as her fictional community, and the action of the story is contained almost entirely within that parish which is socially well represented from the landowner and mill-owner to the mill-worker, and from the rector and the curates to the Sunday-school children. And the influence of near-by parishes, of the manufactories at Stilbro', of political agitation in Manchester and Nottingham are all felt in Briarhead.

The parish is affected also by the conflict between established and dissenting church which is exacerbated by the dissenters' sympathy with industrial unrest, and the established church's with the landowner and mill-owner.

Not only did she make use of actual events of the time, but she included people living in the area of Roe Head at that period. Her method was complicated by making use also of people she knew in Haworth and elsewhere, grafting on to historical characters the characteristics of her contemporaries. Thus the curates are based on the curates she knew at Haworth, Caroline Helstone is her friend Ellen Nussey, Shirley is Emily Brontë as she would have been 'had she been placed in health and prosperity'; the Yorke family was based on the Taylor family.

THE STORY

The plot is a complicated one, since it consists of a number of parallel stories. Although the novel takes its title from one of the characters, that character cannot be said to be the sole protagonist. The novel begins with a not very flattering picture of the curates of the area, and an attack on the new machinery for the mill. It ends in the Victorian welter of marriages and reconciliations.

Caroline Helstone's parents separated soon after her birth and she lives with her uncle, the Reverend Helstone, rector of Briarfield. She is in love with Robert Moore, who is of Flemish and English extraction, and whose father was distantly related to Caroline's mother. Robert's whole concern in life is the success of Hollow's-mill and he is determined to install machinery there to ensure this success. Early in the story an argument between Helstone and Moore results in Caroline being forbidden to visit Hollow's cottage, though even before this she has come to doubt Robert's love for her.

Miss Shirley Keeldar, heiress, landowner in the district and landlord of the mill, arrives with her governess, Mrs. Pryor, to stay for a while at her house, Fieldhead, since she has come of age. A strong friendship springs up between the two girls. Together they witness the attempt by the workers on Hollow's-mill, together they take walks, together they take part in the annual Sunday-school walk and tea-drinking.

Caroline falls into a decline, and is nursed to health by Mrs. Pryor, who turns out to be her long-lost mother. Shirley is visited by her uncle, Mr. Sympson, his family and his son's tutor.

Opposing her uncle's plans to marry her off, and rejecting Robert Moore who wants to marry her for her fortune, Shirley at length confesses to her love for the tutor, Louis Moore, brother of Robert, whom she has loved since she lived with the Sympson family as a girl. Robert Moore, shot by a leader of the workmen, is nursed to health by his friends, the Yorkes, repents his general harshness, and marries Caroline.

EMPHASIS UPON THE INDIVIDUAL

However carefully Charlotte Brontë limits the area of this story in time and place, however carefully she marks political, social and religious influences, the novel is not of the Victorian social reform kind. There is no reforming zeal at work. The brief picture of the child labourers coming to the mill evokes no Dickensian indignation; the poverty of the laid-off workers no Gaskellian pity. As in her other novels, her true concern is with the individual and his private predicament. Only in the case of Robert Moore does she analyse the effect of public events upon the private person, and even here her concern is not with public reform but with the need for personal integrity.

CONCERN WITH ECONOMICS

The economic theme is much more to the fore than it was in *The Professor*, and with a different perspective. As against the personal and domestic concern with economics in the first novel, we have here a story based upon certain political events and industrial advancements which drastically affect national trade and commerce. The result is suffering at the level of the individual person who is powerless to do anything about the causes of his suffering. The strife, bitterness, and unhappiness is seen as affecting the whole of society—there is war between employer and worker, ranting quarrels among the curates, disagreement on religious and political issues among the gentlemen and clergy. The situation can be bettered only by a turn in political events which are outside the influence of the individual. After the repeal of the Orders in Council, 'Stocks . . . went off in a moment . . . warehouses were lightened, ships were laden;

work abounded, wages rose: the good time seemed come. These prospects might be delusive, but they were brilliant—to some they were even true.'

The moral stress upon the individual of such circumstances is presented through the character of Robert Moore. Whereas Crimsworth retained his self-respect and integrity in the face of economic pressure, Robert Moore is corrupted by it. He is on the verge of bankruptcy and to save himself he must install machinery in the mill. In his struggle for survival, poor men such as William Farren must go to the wall: '. . . straitened on all sides as I am, I have nothing for it but to push on . . . for me to pretend to offer a man a livelihood would be to do a dishonest thing.' His love for Caroline Helstone is 'weakness', 'there's downright ruin' in it since she has no fortune to bring him. He turns from her, and proposes to Shirley, the rich heiress. Moore is brought, through Shirley's rejection of him and his subsequent wanderings in England, to realise the nature of his corruption. In his long conversation with Yorke, he admits to rejecting Caroline—the true match for him because of their shared interest, their common love and understanding—to court another for her wealth, even though Shirley 'never crept into [his] heart or influenced its pulse'. And he admits that, while he would still fight a 'riotous mob' of workmen, he can sympathise with their plight to the extent of looking beyond his personal interest, beyond the advancement of well-laid schemes—'To respect himself, a man must believe he renders justice to his fellow-men.'

Shirley is central to this theme since she is a rich heiress. Robert Moore, two of the curates, and several gentlemen in the neighbourhood become interested in marrying her because of her fortune: 'It appeared that Miss Keeldar—or her fortune—had by this time made a sensation in the district.' Money and money-making are seen as corrupting influences and hence there is a certain uneasiness about Shirley's wealth—she gives much to charity, constantly loses her keys to the place where her money is kept and finds herself without sixpence, argues with one of the curates when he berates her for donating only five pounds to charity. Louis Moore sees gold as a Griffin guarding Shirley.

The economic theme, as it applies to the love affair of Shirley and Louis Moore, is a reversal of the *Jane Eyre* situation. Wealth and position are on the side of the woman, the man is poor both economically and in social status.

THE FEMINIST THEME

Although a concern with the position of women in society and the kinds of lives they lead is implicit in her other novels, it is only in *Shirley* that it becomes a predominant theme centring on the lives of the two heroines, Caroline and Shirley.

In *The Professor*, the idea of women having useful work to do and holding positions of authority and independence existed in Mademoiselle Reuter as Directress of a school, and in Mademoiselle Henri's similar position later in the novel. Even in *Jane Eyre*, Jane as governess and heiress is independent, and the possibility of Jane becoming a man's plaything and mistress is rejected. And in *Jane Eyre* there is at least one forceful passage on the position of women which has little relevance at that point to the story and which springs from Charlotte's conviction that women need useful and purposeful occupations:

> Women are supposed to be very calm generally: but women feel just as men feel; they need exercise for their faculties, and a field for their efforts as much as their brothers do . . . it is narrow-minded . . . to say that they ought to confine themselves to making puddings and knitting stockings . . .   Chapter 12

And the alternative to marriage—the barren life of an old maid— is touched upon by Frances in *The Professor*:

> An old maid's life must doubtless be void and vapid—her heart strained and empty. Had I been an old maid I should have spent existence in efforts to fill the void and ease the aching. I should have probably failed, and died weary and disappointed, despised and of no account, like other single women.   Chapter XXV

This concern comes out most strongly in the character of Caroline Helstone. Caroline is caught in the dilemma of the

Victorian woman. Realising that Robert Moore will not marry her, she reflects: 'Till lately I had reckoned securely on the duties and affections of wife and mother to occupy my existence. I considered . . . that I was growing up to the ordinary destiny . . . but now, I perceive plainly, I may have been mistaken. Probably I shall be an old maid' (Chapter X). Faced with this possibility, Caroline looks into the position of old maids, and their activities. Fundamentally, the plea is for the recognition of honourable occupations for unmarried women so that they may lead a satisfying and fulfilled existence. Caroline makes strenuous attempts to fill in her days with visiting, walking, charitable concerns, but they provide no sense of fulfilment. Her uncle recommends the accepted 'time-fillers' for women, treating them as empty-headed creatures—a new frock, a visit to a watering-place. He cannot see why his niece should wish to go out as a governess when she has all she needs and will be provided with an annuity when he dies. He concludes by advising her to 'run away and amuse' herself, and ironically she ponders: 'What with? My doll?' 'I believe single women should have more to do—better chances of interesting and profitable occupation than they possess now,' she concludes.

Women are allowed no satisfactory public life, unless such things as visiting and a Sunday-school tea-drinking can be so considered. But men are able to have a private and a public life, and thus lead a full existence. Unhappiness does not weigh on them—they have their business or profession to occupy their thoughts. It is the objection made by Anne Elliot in *Persuasion*, and one of the reasons for Caroline's demands that a woman should be allowed an occupation. 'Different, indeed, is Robert's mental condition to mine: [Caroline concludes] I think only of him, he has no room, no leisure to think of me.'

Caroline Helstone's lack of character, her long, brooding inactivity in the novel, her serious illness, are as much the result of the weariness of life without purpose of an unmarried woman as of the sorrowing and decline of the girl crossed in love.

Shirley is, of course, above such worries, and is shown to have much to occupy her, but even so, a comparison of the occupations of the two girls (Chapter XXII) reveals a great deal of similarity, and Shirley's pursuits are quite as trivial in some ways as those of Caroline. Fundamentally, it is Shirley's nature which enables her to find such restrictions of activity not irksome.

In any case, Charlotte Brontë offers no solution to the feminist problem in this book. Shirley, the landowner, farmer, millowner and heiress, abdicates wealth, position and power in favour of her husband; Caroline marries Robert Moore and the problems of unmarried life are removed from her. But a third attitude to the feminine dilemma is suggested by the young girl, Rose Yorke, in her determination to use the talents God gave her and not bury them in a life of domesticity.

THE MASTER–PUPIL RELATIONSHIP

The movement towards a happy marriage has previously formed the converging point of all other themes in her novels. It is not so here, where there is no sense of a gradual and growing understanding between partners. Between Shirley and Louis Moore, there is an attempt to present such development, but we are *informed* that it exists rather than seeing it and experiencing it as it happens. And in the case of Shirley's marriage to Louis Moore, the master–pupil relationship is dragged in by the ears and stretched and tugged to fit over a pattern which is entirely different. Shirley, independent and superior in position to Louis, can only be seen in the pupil relationship in terms of superior learning on his part. The pattern of growth and understanding does not exist. Hence those repeated scenes in which Louis Moore commands her, as her teacher, to return to her position as his pupil, and where the relationship remains on this level as he teaches her French or makes her recite poetry.

It is interesting that Louis Moore, talking to Shirley of the woman he would like to marry, brings in an imaginary situation which involves the more usual Charlotte-heroine and her relationship to her future husband. He wishes he could find 'some young penniless, friendless orphan girl . . . not uneducated— honest and modest . . . I would fain have the germ of those sweet natural powers which nothing acquired can rival: any temper

Fate wills,—I can manage the hottest. To such a creature as this, I should like to be first tutor and then husband'.

Furthermore, there is a development of another aspect of the marriage theme which has only been hinted at previously. The book is filled with unhappy marriages—marriages in which it is the woman who comes off worst—and this is closely related to the feminine theme, both involving a man's view of woman.

In *Shirley*, the men generally are unwilling to accept women as equal and intelligent partners. A woman like Shirley is looked upon as a good match because of her money. Helstone prefers women who are light-headed so that he can see them as his inferiors. His wife pined away almost unnoticed—he believes that people tire of one another in marriage. Mrs. Pryor comments: '. . . life is an illusion . . . Most of the cheats of existence are strong . . . [the] sweetness [of love] is . . . transitory.'

Shirley gives her opinion as to how one may judge the right mate, by observing his behaviour with others, with those weaker and more helpless than himself, by observing his attitude to women. But this is a minority view in face of all the opinions raised against marriage in the novel.

GROUPING OF CHARACTERS

We have seen how, in earlier novels, characters have been grouped according to theme. In *Shirley* it would seem that they are grouped according to sex, and in this way are linked with all the themes that have been shown to exist in the novel. Thus the men are strong characters, dominant in public and private life, individualistic. They function in public life as clergy, landowners, tradesmen. Main events in the novel are those involving men— the attack on the mill can only be observed at a distance by Shirley, landowner though she may be. Mr. Helstone asks her to stay with his niece that night without thinking it necessary to explain the state of affairs. Even on the level of the working-class men, this grouping can be seen. When Shirley attempts to talk political economy with Joe, the working man, no communication is possible: ' "Joe, do you seriously think all the wisdom in the world is lodged in male skulls?" . . . " . . . women is to take their husbands' opinion, both in politics and religion: it's whole-somest for them." ' And William, when Shirley asks what she can do about the condition of the poor replies: 'Do?—ye can do naught mich, poor young lass! Ye've gi'en your brass . . .'

Set against the men are the women, seen as old maids, young girls with their sights set on marriage, housewives, either married or single. Of these, the latter are in some ways most content—Mrs. Yorke and Hortense Moore have their household duties to occupy them. Miss Mann and Miss Ainley find their satisfaction in good works of a charitable kind, but under the dominance of male direction. Young girls lead idle existences hoping to marry eventually.

Shirley is an attempt on a woman's part to straddle the two groupings. She is a woman who, through birth and position, occupies many of the posts normally filled by men; she refers to herself as Captain Keeldar. But it is noticeable that she is a figure-head in her position as landowner. She has more authority, more intimacy with business concerns than Caroline, but at crucial moments in political events she must retain the passive role of a woman.

PRIVATE GRIEF—THEME THROUGH IMAGERY AND REFLECTION

An underlying theme of the novel is the need to endure suffering stoically and without much hope, and this theme is presented not so much in terms of the action as through the imagery and reflections on life from both characters and author. The only panacea offered is that the passage of time and changing circum-stances will modify pain. When Caroline Helstone begins to feel that Robert does not return her love, we have several images of extreme and violent suffering: 'You expected bread, and you have got a stone; break your teeth on it, and don't shriek because the nerves are martyrised . . .' There follow the images of the arm swollen from the scorpion's sting, the body stretched on the rack. The moral is 'endure without a sob', for 'if you survive the test . . . you will be stronger, wiser, less sensitive . . . Nature leaving a convenient stoicism', a half-bitter stoicism, but 'bitter-ness is strength' (Chapter VII).

Mrs. Pryor, praying for the survival of Caroline, has her prayers answered and Caroline restored to health, but the opposite result is suggested with great poignancy:

> Night after night the sweat of agony may burst dark on the forehead; the supplicant may cry for mercy . . . Then the watcher . . . feels at once that the insufferable moment draws nigh, knows that it is God's will his idol shall be broken . . . and subdues his soul to the sentence he cannot avert . . .   Chapter XXV

Louis Moore reflects that his pupil must learn 'to take [his] share of the bitter of life with all of Adam's race . . .' Caroline, thinking of unhappiness on earth, can only conclude that 'God hears many a groan . . . which man stops his ears against'. Poverty among the mill workers is seen as 'the will of God . . . but He tries us to the utmost'. This silent acceptance of suffering is seen also in the case of Shirley when she is bitten by a mad dog, and Louis Moore when he is ill with fever. Particularly, such ideas centre on Caroline, who concludes 'Life is short . . . seventy years, they say, pass like a vapour . . . every path trod by human feet terminates in one bourne—the grave . . . The soul's real hereafter, who shall guess?'

Whereas in *The Professor* there was no intense or unbearable suffering or unhappiness, little temptation that could not be overcome, and in *Jane Eyre* suffering and sin were ultimately ended and forgiven, in *Shirley* there is constant reminder of the suffering of mankind which God, who seems to have withdrawn to a great distance, appears to overlook. There is little sense of happiness on this earth that is not fortuitous, and certain doubts about its existence in Heaven.

But the reflections upon such suffering and the need for stoicism do not function within the action of the novel. Caroline, although she suffers for a time, has her mother returned to her, and wins Robert's love. Mrs. Pryor prays for her daughter's return to health, and her prayer is granted. The bitterness that comes through suffering unalleviated, prayers not answered, which the authorial commentary carries, is not demonstrated in the action, but is a subdued commentary upon human life in general, its harshness, and the inexplicableness of suffering.

On the other hand, there is a great deal of religion in the novel —religion of a worldly kind. The church is well represented through its curates and ministers, though the curates are only interested in food, drink, argument, and finding wives, and one of the rectors, Mr. Helstone, treated his wife with cruelty, and missed his real vocation of the army. He is prepared to carry arms against his parishioners. There is the charity of the Jew-basket and the charity of Shirley, but there is also the sense of a religion offering little hope, of clergy dedicated to worldly pursuits, of long, boring talks and Sunday observance. Nor do the Methodists offer an alternative—they are shown as hypocrites, ranters, and stirrers-up of the working-people. Shirley herself stays outside church on the day of the Sunday-school tea-drinking to avoid the heat and boredom within and to enjoy the beauty of nature without. But Shirley is pagan.

SENSE OF PLACE

Shirley is not so successful as a novel in spite of all Charlotte's care in the planning and writing of it. Perhaps her own unhappiness at her sisters' deaths and a feeling of dissatisfaction with her life generally at that time are responsible for the failure. The lesser emotional involvement on her part can be seen from a comparison of two passages—one from *Jane Eyre*, the other from *Shirley*. Although the sense of place is strong in this novel—that is, the sense of a specific and provincial area with its scenery, history, character, peoples, and dialect—the physical background is not vividly actualised, and it remains tied to the realism of the novel.

In *Jane Eyre* the setting varies according to the stage of Jane's pilgrimage which has been reached, the language and treatment generally lifting it on to a symbolic plane, the symbols pointing constantly towards the religious and moral themes that are being worked out. Thus, Jane, wandering on the moor, describes what is obviously the Yorkshire moorland, but its emptiness becomes symbolic of her loneliness, her rejection of human society in her anguish, and of her turning to nature for protection and through nature to God:

High banks of moor were about me; the crag protected my head: the sky was over that ... calmed by the deep silence that reigned as evening declined at nightfall, I took confidence ... I touched the heath: it was dry and yet warm with the heat of the summer day ... a kindly star twinkled just above the chasm ridge. The dew fell, but with propitious softness ... Nature seemed to be benign and good ...

On the other hand, the description of Nunnwood in *Shirley* (Chapter XL) lacks this sense of the personally observed, and is limited in its connotations by the use of conventional language of description—'sylvan chase' 'robed in May raiment', 'azury snow'. At the same time, it is tied firmly to the specific by the use of proper names, and its relationship to British history and to Yorkshire:

... they looked down on the deep valley robed in May raiment; on varied meads, some pearled with daisies, and some golden with king-cups ... On Nunnwood—the sole remnant of antique British forest in a region whose lowlands were once all sylvan chase, as its highlands were breast-deep heather—slept the shadow of a cloud ... silvery blues, soft purples, evanescent greens ... all melting into fleeces of white cloud ... pure as azury snow, allured the eye ... 'Our England is a bonnie island,' said Shirley, 'and Yorkshire is one of her bonniest nooks.'

NARRATIVE TECHNIQUE

The story is told in the third person—a further departure from the earlier novels. Although the material she had selected could hardly have been presented in any other way, yet by removing a central, feeling conscience from the novel she cuts herself off from her main strength. Furthermore, she deliberately, as in *The Professor*, sets out to tell a realistic story, eschewing once more imagination. It is significant that, as in *The Professor*, she again unhappily attempts to dissuade her reader from proceeding with the tale:

If you think, from this prelude, that anything like a romance is preparing for you, reader, you never were more mistaken. Do you anticipate sentiment, and poetry, and reverie? Do you expect

> passion, and stimulus, and melodrama? Calm your expectation;
> reduce them to a lowly standard. Something real, cool, and solid,
> lies before you; something unromantic as Monday morning . . .
>
> Chapter I

This is a different attitude from that of *Jane Eyre* or *Villette*, where the drawing of the reader into the convincing fictional world is the major concern of the novel. And her uneasiness with her material further reveals itself in the customary exaggeration of the Brontë faults—high rhetoric, addresses to the reader, superabundant imagery, and a false emphasis on certain aspects of the story.

In this novel, as in *The Professor*, there is a lack of proportion in presenting character and events. Even in terms of her special method of construction, which we observed in *Jane Eyre*, we cannot justify the great detail expended on the Yorke family; the duplication of the go-between situation of Martin Yorke and Henry Sympson; the lack of certainty in the introduction of Shirley's essay—which ought never to have been written, let alone repeated; Louis Moore's burblings to his diary on the subject of love; the set pieces on the spinsters; the set pieces between Shirley and the workmen. Scenes frequently lack any vital emotion or intention, and the dialogue is frequently un-dynamic (e.g. the scene in the school-room, Chapter XXVI).

Unfortunately, Charlotte is caught up here in intentions which cannot be successfully portrayed in fiction. Shirley is intended to have greater insight into what is going on than everyone else, but since she does not reveal her insights until a situation has been revealed to her, she is unconvincing. The attempt to portray the Charlotte-heroine in fortunate circumstances as well as the attempt to analyse the situation of the unmarried woman is unsuccessful because both, by their nature, are dogged by lack of appropriate action.

Finally, Charlotte in this novel, to a greater extent than in *Jane Eyre*, sets up moral, spiritual and social problems, such as the position of women, but evades a solution to the complications by dropping the problem and substituting the conventional solution of marriage.

84

6

Villette

'*Jane Eyre* was not written under such circumstances, nor were two-thirds of *Shirley*. I got so miserable about it, I could bear no allusion to the book.' So Charlotte Brontë wrote to her publishers about her last novel, *Villette*, which was finished in November 1852. The different circumstances she refers to were those of having no opinion besides her own on the book, 'no one to whom to read a line, or of whom to ask a counsel'. Since the writing of *Shirley*, not only had she experienced an increased isolation and loneliness through the loss of her sisters, but she also suffered nervously and physically from these circumstances. Yet *Villette* was received with acclamation—wondered at because out of 'so small a circle of characters, dwelling in so dull and monotonous an area as a "pension", this wonderful tale' had been evolved.

For subject-matter and setting, she had returned to *The Professor*, to the teaching life and her Brussels experience, and it is more obvious in this novel than in *The Professor* that she is drawing particularly upon the intimate emotional experience of that part of her life. The love between master and pupil in her first novel was obviously based upon her abortive love for M. Heger. In *Villette*, the situation is re-worked with its strength drawn from that past love of hers and the perspective placed firmly, where it was in real life, in the female part of the relationship.

Lucy's love for M. Paul Emanuel in the novel is, in spite of the attempts to prevent it, returned by him. 'It kills me to be forgotten, monsieur,' Lucy tells him. 'All these weary days I have not heard from you one word, and I was crushed with the possibility, growing to certainty, that you would depart without saying farewell.' M. Paul gives Lucy proof of his love, but M. Heger, after limiting the number of letters Charlotte might write to him, eventually ended the correspondence. Her last letter to him reveals the misery she suffered: 'If my master withdraws his friendship from me entirely I shall be altogether without hope; if he gives me a little—just a little—I shall be satisfied—happy . . . Monsieur, the poor have not need of much to sustain them—they ask only for the crumbs that fall from the rich man's table.'

She returned also in this novel to the limits of realism she had set herself in her first and third novels, and with greater success. There is, no doubt, the ghostly and Gothic figure of the nun, though this is given a rational, if unlikely, explanation eventually. The mechanics of the plot depend to an impossible extent upon coincidence, but much of the novel is a skilful presentation of a personal drama growing out of the prosaic events of school life.

Villette, like *Jane Eyre*, deals with the life of a woman who is obscure, plain, poor, and an orphan. The story is seen through her eyes, and it shows her efforts to achieve independence and love. But it differs fundamentally from *Jane Eyre* not only in its basic realism but also in the character of its heroine. Lucy Snowe has not Jane's passion, certainty, decision, and ability to live for the present moment. The most striking development in *Villette* lies in the character of Lucy, whose constant and speculative inner monologue upon the nature and variety of the human condition produces a novel of inquiry and analysis rather than of certainty and demonstration. Nor does Lucy need to be involved in exciting melodrama to bring out her sterling qualities. The most ordinary events of life are sufficient to test and develop her character.

'SUCH WAS GOD'S WILL CONCERNING THEM'

The conception behind the novel is again the pilgrimage through life, and Bunyan is referred to in the first chapter: 'My visits to [my godmother] resembled the sojourn of Christian and Hopeful beside a certain pleasant stream.' Lucy's pilgrimage is seen in relation to that theory which Charlotte had mentioned to Mrs. Gaskell 'that it did not fall to the lot of all . . . to have their lines fall in pleasant places'; some 'had rougher paths' to follow, and they must 'perceive that such was God's will concerning them', and try to 'moderate their expectations' and seek 'patience and resignation'. At the end of Chapter 33 of the novel, this theme is clearly stated, when Lucy writes of Paulina and Dr. John: 'Some lives *are* thus blessed: it is God's will: it is the attesting trace and lingering evidence of Eden. Other lives run from the first another course . . . Neither can this happen without the sanction of God.'

Thus, Lucy Snowe's path in life seems doomed to be unpleasant and dreary: 'When I had full leisure to look on life as life must be looked on by such as me, I found it but a hopeless desert.' The story follows Lucy's development from girlhood to maturity, tracing the path in life that is preordained for her, and revealing her efforts to come to terms with her fate.

But linked with this idea of fate is the nature and temperament of the pilgrim, which is again 'given' but which can be matured or frustrated by the circumstances in which he is placed. Writing to George Smith in 1851, and referring to the 'Phrenological Character' she had taken in his company, Charlotte reflects:

> . . . perhaps few dwell upon a friend's capacity for the intellectual, or care how this might expand, if there were but facilities allowed for cultivation, and space given for growth. It seems to me that, even *should such space and facilities be denied by stringent circumstances and a rigid fate*, still it should do you good fully to know, and tenaciously to remember, that you have such a capacity.
>
> MRS. GASKELL, Chapter XXIII [my italics]

Lucy Snowe is aware throughout her pilgrimage of the dual concerns of one's fate and one's nature, and how precariously one is balanced between happiness and sorrow, fulfilment and frustration. She tells Paulina Home: 'As a child I feared for you; nothing that has life was ever more susceptible than your nature in infancy . . . Much pain, much fear, much struggle . . . would have harassed your nerves into the fever of habitual irritation . . . Providence has protected and cultured you . . .'

The individual is, however, in spite of such predetermination, left with some space for manœuvre, as Charlotte said—acceptance of one's lot united with faith in God's decision, and an attempt to live as fully as possible within the limits set.

LUCY SNOWE—THE COMPROMISE WITH FATE

'As to the name of the heroine . . . A *cold* name she must have . . . she has about her an external coldness . . . You say that she may be thought morbid and weak . . . I consider that she *is* both morbid and weak at times . . .' This was Charlotte's opinion as she gave it to her publishers. Lucy Snowe begins in reserve and lack of passion. The early chapters describe her visit to her godmother, Mrs. Bretton. There she enjoys peace and lack of stimulus: '. . . I liked peace so well, and sought stimulus so little, that when the latter came I almost felt it a disturbance, and wished rather it had still held aloof.' The simultaneous visit of a child, Paulina Mary Home, while her father is travelling abroad, allows Lucy to take up the role of the looker-on, the calm, detached observer of the working of a totally opposed nature, Paulina's reactions to her father and to John Graham Bretton are intensely emotional.

There follows for Lucy a period of suffering which is not particularised and which concludes with her obtaining a post as companion to a single lady, Miss Marchmont. This service suits her nature: 'All within me became narrowed to my lot.' 'Tame and still by habit, disciplined by destiny,' she wishes only to compromise with fate, 'to escape occasional great agonies by submitting to a whole life of privation and small pains'.

The first stirrings of Lucy's buried nature are seen in the urge to travel which she feels after the death of Miss Marchmont. This urge takes her as far as Madame Beck's pensionnat in Villette, a town in Labassecour on the continent. She finds work there as nursery maid to Madame Beck's children, and her former attitude regains ascendancy. Ensconced in the 'watch-tower' of the nursery at the Rue D'Isabelle, she would have done nothing to move out into the world; 'the negation of severe suffering was the nearest approach to happiness I expected to know'.

But 'negation of suffering' is not to be allowed her. She is forced out of her 'watch-tower' by Madame Beck who needs an English teacher. The incident forms a crisis in Lucy's life, for she is fully aware of the difficulties and emotional trials she is faced with. Agitated at her own weakness, her lack of French, and the prospect of facing the most difficult of the classes, the numerous, unmanageable second division, she is 'tremulous from head to foot'. Madame Beck's stern question as Lucy trembles at the door to the classroom is meaningful: 'Will you go forward or back?' Thus challenged, Lucy goes forward, gives the lesson, overcomes her difficulties, and enters a new stage of her existence.

Part of her nature is now satisfied—she is learning and teaching: 'Experience of a certain kind' lies before her, her time is now 'well and profitably filled up', she is not stagnating. But that aspect of her nature which desires a wider and more satisfying existence, love and affection, is repressed: 'in catalepsy and a dead trance, I studiously held the quick of my nature'.

NERVOUS BREAKDOWN

A second, and major crisis, occurs when, during the long vacation, Lucy is left in isolation and loneliness at the school. With the 'prop of employment' withdrawn, depression at her situation in life makes her ill: 'A sorrowful indifference to existence often pressed on me . . . the conviction would grasp me that Fate was my permanent foe . . . I concluded it to be part of His great plan that some must deeply suffer while they live, and I thrilled in the certainty that of this number, I was one.'

Goaded by fever and restlessness, Lucy wanders through Villette, and eventually goes to confession at a Catholic church. The priest sees this action of hers as a call from God to her to become Catholic, and interprets her nature as of the kind that makes penitents here, their recompense coming in the next life.

Lucy resists such persuasions, but 'the mere relief of communication' had done her good.

After leaving the church, she collapses, and recovers to find herself in the house of Dr. John, the school doctor, whom she has already recognised as Graham Bretton. Lucy is thus reunited with her godmother, Mrs. Bretton, and is no longer without some friends.

Her life now changes. Through her friendship with the Brettons she begins to live more fully, to see more of society—her life does not want variety. A belief in happiness begins to grow in her, along with love for Dr. John, but she is, all the time, aware of the danger of relying too much on this new friendship. By another coincidence, the Homes, father and daughter, are met with again, and Lucy, seeing that the love of Paulina and Dr. John for each other is a foregone conclusion, stifles her affection for him.

She does not return to melancholy, though. A major turning point for her is the moment when she can face the likelihood of a future in which there will be nothing beyond herself to love. Accepting this, she makes plans for starting a school of her own, seeking at least some object in life, a field in which to exercise her talents.

M. PAUL

But this decision is taken just after M. Paul has looked after her while she slept, and this action of his is indicative of his growing affection for her. Their love develops and in spite of obstacles put in their way, they come together. With M. Paul, Lucy is able to reveal her true nature, which flowers under his protection. She can give her confidence and love, be happy in the knowledge of his love for her, and work contentedly within the limits life has set for her. Even though they have to part when he leaves for the West Indies, she experiences 'a new state of circumstances, a relieved heart'. And while he is absent she 'was not suffered to fear penury; [she] was not tried with suspense. By every vessel he wrote: he wrote as he gave and as he loved, in full-handed, full-hearted plenitude.'

In the course of this love, Lucy is to suffer the great agonies she sought to avoid, she is to suffer jealousy, and she is ultimately to lose Paul, but, whatever appearances may be, she is no longer a looker-on at life, life is not 'a hopeless desert' for her, she has felt and experienced to the full measure of her nature.

Lucy Snowe's development from coldness and timidity, in the face of her own nature and the world, to love and a willingness to accept life's experiences is the central concern of the novel. It offers a more optimistic view of life than that presented in *Shirley*, in that no forcible wrenching of the plot to a happy conclusion is needed. Lucy has her love, her three years of happiness and hope. If after that she has her sorrow, she will, presumably, have learnt to come to terms with it. Charlotte Brontë has gone beyond the complacency of *The Professor*, the spiritual melodrama of *Jane Eyre*, the bitter hopelessness of *Shirley*. In this novel, the most significant feeling is the return to the assurance of God's will being at work, however inexplicably; to the acceptance of one's lot in life without bitterness, without too much hope of heavenly reward, but with calmness and the determination to make the most of what is given.

IMPORTANCE OF THE INSIGNIFICANT, REALISTIC EVENT

In returning to the 'real' world for her material, Charlotte Brontë shows herself in this novel much more skilled as a writer. She is able now, as she was not in *Shirley*, to take an incident which is, in itself, of minor importance, and develop it successfully into a significant event in the scheme of the novel. Most frequently, it is some aspect of school life which is the basis of such development.

There is, for example, the occasion of M. Paul's fête. This is deliberately contrasted with that of Madame Beck. In conformity with their characters, hers is 'plotted and contrived beforehand', his is 'an honour spontaneously awarded'. The mood of anticipation is simply, but effectively, set in the classes with their tribute of flowers, and Lucy's empty hands. The simple ceremony of presentation begins:

> The long train of offerings followed: all the pupils, sweeping past with the gliding step foreigners practise, left their tributes as they

went by. Each girl so dextrously adjusted her separate gift, that when the last bouquet was laid on the desk, it formed the apex of a blooming pyramid . . . This ceremony over . . . we sat in dead silence, expectant of a speech.

There follows M. Paul's tragically repeated, 'Est-ce-là tout?' expressive of his disbelief and disappointment that Lucy should have failed to bring him a flower; his gulping down of his disappointment and the commencement of his 'discours'. This is interrupted by Lucy dropping her thimble, which interruption launches him into invective against the English, which rouses Lucy's cry of 'Vive l'Angleterre!' Nothing here is melodramatic, and the incident is of no significance in itself. It gains significance from the revelation of the feelings of the two protagonists, their attachment to each other, their perverseness and nervous irritation at a slight, and their opposing characters. The setting and sense of school life are vividly recalled.

The opposition to their growing love is portrayed in a similarly simple and unpretentious way. Lucy, waiting in the second division with her books, papers and pens ready for a lesson with M. Paul, sees him busy in the carré. He is good-humoured with others, carefully tends the plants there, speaks endearments to the dog. She waits, patiently. The moon rises. M. Paul 'suddenly looked round . . . I think he bowed . . . In a moment he was gone . . . Gathering in my arms all that was spread on the desk before me, I carried back the unused heap to its place in the third classe.' The incident, a trivial happening on one evening, carries within it all Lucy's expectations and disappointment, the opposition in situation and temperament between them. She, typically, is in the solitary classe, alone, shadowed, expectant of some small pleasure and a friend's company. M. Paul is in the carré where the setting sun casts a warm light, where he is the centre of a busy throng, surrounded by orange trees, cacti, camelias. Appropriately, he cannot come to Lucy and bring some of this warmth and colour to her.

Lucy's visit to the Catholic church—a climax for her, a staunch Protestant, and coming after several weeks of growing unhappiness—is still presented concisely and without melodrama:

Few worshippers were assembled, and, the *salut* over, half of them departed . . . I did not stir . . . a holy quiet sank upon, and a solemn shade gathered about us. After a space, breathless and spent in prayer . . . A pale lady, kneeling near me, said in a low, kind voice:

'Go you now, I am not quite prepared.'

Mechanically obedient, I rose and went . . .

The priest within the confessional never turned his eyes to regard me: he only quietly inclined his ear to my lips. He might be a good man, but this duty had become to him a sort of form . . . I hesitated . . . I said:

'Mon père, je suis Protestante.'

CHARACTER

The novel is not intended as a militant justification of the heroine's thoughts and actions, and this follows from the change of theme. An inquiry into the various lives of the characters, a study of their different natures with regard only to the effect of one upon the other does not necessitate propaganda. And so character is no longer flat, as it was in *The Professor*; nor made convincing but larger than life through a melodramatic presentation of one aspect, as it was in *Jane Eyre*; nor limited to one stance and one reaction to life, as it was in *Shirley*.

There is a sense of the diversity of human nature. Mrs. Bretton and her son have 'spirits of that tone and equality which are better than a fortune to the possessors', 'human tempers, bland, glowing, and genial' which like 'to communicate happiness . . . they did it instinctively'. Paulina Home has 'a one-idead nature . . . the most unfortunate with which man or woman can be cursed' but Fate is kind to her and her life is happy. Madame Beck is 'Wise, firm, faithless; secret, crafty, passionless; watchful and inscrutable; acute and insensate'; 'she ought to have swayed a nation . . . In her own single person she could have comprised the duties of a first minister and a superintendent of police.' The King of Labassecour is haunted by 'constitutional melancholy'.

But there is also an awareness in the novel of the lights and shades of individual character, of private hopes and fears and reactions to life. The development in Lucy Snowe, revealed in her deepening understanding of M. Paul's nature, is, of course, central. But understanding is extended to others. Mme Beck, imagining for a time that Dr. John might love her, suddenly realises that this is not possible: 'When he was gone, Madame dropped into the chair . . . all that was animated and amiable vanished from her face: she looked stony and stern, almost mortified and morose . . . She got up; as she passed a dressing-table with a glass upon it, she looked at her reflected image. One single white hair streaked her nut brown tresses; she plucked it out with a shudder.' Strange little woman, reflects Lucy, wondering at Madame's nature. Dr. John, devoted doctor and cultured man as he is, yet has 'cruel vanity' and 'sometime levity', 'his passing passion for that present; shown . . . selfishly, by extracting from it whatever it could yield of nutriment to his masculine self-love'.

Relationships between characters in this novel are also more convincingly presented, frequently through Charlotte's greater skill at dialogue which here is varied and suited to character. The relationship between Mrs. Bretton and her son, at its level, has none of the woodenness of that between Crimsworth and Yorke Hunsden—she can suggest an intimacy without stridency or sentimentality.

MORAL TOLERANCE

We do not find in the novel, of course, the psychological subtlety of a George Eliot, or the ironical perception of a Jane Austen, but we do have a greater moral tolerance in the face of diverse human nature. True, there are some sweeping moral comments: 'to the wicked [perfect happiness] never comes': 'often [the fortunate] are not pampered, selfish beings, but Nature's elect, harmonious and benign; men and women mild with charity, kind agents of God's kind attributes'; and to Madame Beck, Lucy cries: 'Keep your hand off me, and my life, and my troubles . . . in *your* hand there is both chill and poison. You envenom and you paralyse.' But there is, generally, a greater appreciation of the moral lights and shades of character, and a greater tolerance of them. Lucy, speaking of Ginevra, comments on 'that directness which was her best point . . . which was, in short, the salt, the sole preservative ingredient of a character otherwise not formed to keep'. There is understanding, but no condemnation, of Ginevra and her way of getting through life: 'Under every cloud . . . Ginevra . . . called out lustily for sympathy and aid . . . and so she got on fighting the battle of life by proxy, and, on the whole, suffering as little as any human being I have ever known.'

This new sense of justice to individual natures is seen particularly in relation to the habit of 'surveillance' which Madame Beck and her relative M. Paul both indulge in. Lucy disapproves of this, but on several occasions she catches one or other of them at it without launching into condemnation. There is rather a sense of humour playing over the incidents: 'The sound of a drawer cautiously slid out struck my ear . . . Very good. A dumpy, motherly, little body, in decent shawl and the cleanest of possible nightcaps, stood before this toilet, hard at work . . . not an article . . . but was lifted and unfolded, not a paper but was glanced over, not a little box but was unlidded . . .' On another occasion M. Paul 'occupied my chair; his olive hand held my desk open, his nose was lost to view amongst my papers'.

There is also in this novel a sense of characters existing in their own right apart from the heroine. Ginevra, Madame Beck, the Homes and Brettons all appear to have lives and activities of their own which Lucy impinges upon only at certain intervals. This sense of life going on about her is linked with the way in which character is presented gradually, in a developing fashion, to her understanding, and does not appear ready made and complete. M. Paul is the best example of this, starting as he does as 'A dark little man . . . pungent and austere' coming upon her suddenly with the demand: 'Meess . . ., play you must: I am planted here', to her full realisation of the goodness of his nature.

MASTER–PUPIL RELATIONSHIP

In this novel the master–pupil relationship is developed in its most convincing form, most convincing because the growing towards mutual understanding is demonstrated dramatically, not stated as a theory of relationship. M. Paul and Lucy are different

95

characters, inevitably getting on the wrong side of each other. They fall out over a birthday gift, over sitting together at a table. Superficially, they misunderstand each other's natures. M. Paul suspects Lucy of intellectual pride and of ability she does not have. To her he is vain, irritable, tyrannical and loving public display.

Their relationship leads them through all possible contacts between two people, from the superficial ones, to those springing from natural differences in character, to those lying in religious belief. Each stage in the growth of their relationship is carefully demonstrated and marked, and rises naturally from the public and private events they are involved in. The course of their relationship, even when they reach amity, does not run smoothly, though it runs inevitably, because there is an affinity between them: 'I . . . believe that you were born under my star . . . Tremble! for where that is the case with mortals, the threads of their destinies are difficult to disentangle . . .'

But the final relationship is the traditional one for Charlotte Brontë, with the man as kindly master, the woman as his equal, but acknowledging his superiority. He is the 'benefactor-guest', 'Monsieur'; she is his steward.

As in other examples of this relationship, their love has been tried, in this case by religious pressures, family influence, and separation. But more successfully than in other novels, she has been able to show two different natures gradually coming together in mutual understanding and trust, and whatever trials they have overcome have been in terms of their individual natures and trust in one another.

A NOVEL OF SOCIETY

In *The Professor* and *Jane Eyre* there is little sense of society. The world of school, the immediate world of a large house, are the only attempts to create such a sense. *Villette* is different in that, although events are seen through the eyes of one individual and her life is central to the story, the life and society of the school and the city are very much present in the book. Fundamentally, we must view the novel as one of society, perhaps influenced by

Vanity Fair, certainly developing from *Shirley*, and, just as the change of interest there demanded a wider canvas, so the inquiry into human nature here demands that the novel take in a wider range of human types. Villette—little town—is the world in miniature, and it is through this world that Lucy gains experience.

The world of the novel is Lucy's world—it expands and changes with her development and experience. Lucy's worlds are, to begin with, narrow. The 'allée défendue' in the school garden she makes her own—it is hers in actuality and in symbol—for Lucy's world is then as sequestered and isolated as this alley, her nature is just as repressed and concealed. It is a 'straight and narrow path' where grow some 'tintless flowers'. Sitting here, Lucy is first made aware of a world beyond the school: in hearing the 'far off sounds of the city . . . Quite near were wide streets brightly lit, teeming at this moment with life.'

The school world begins to open for her with Madame's fête. The arrival of the 'coiffeur' and his setting up shop in the oratory, the emphasis upon appearance and dress, the ball, the guests, Ginevra's love affairs, introduce the wider world for the first time to Lucy Snowe—the kind of world she is never really to be a part of.

After her meeting with her godmother again, Lucy's world widens to include life at a château, at an hotel, at theatres, concerts, galleries. She penetrates to the confessional, to the old world of Villette through Père Silas and Madame Walverens.

Intrigue, love, the regulations of class, art, drama, the action of the mob, cold selfishness, grasping interests, loyalty—all of these aspects of human life Lucy is able to view. The court of Villette, with its ceremony and protocol, is merely a 'compact little minor European court, whose very formalities are little more imposing than familiarities'. The fire at the theatrical performance reveals the selfishness in human nature.

It is significant that the climax of Lucy's suffering, the attempt to keep her from M. Paul even to the extent of drugging her, only rouses her to go out into the world; and in a state of greater anguish than she has known, Lucy sees all the significant characters of the novels in representative groups, against the background of a social gathering which is distinctly Villettian: 'In past days there had been, said history, an awful crisis in the fate of Labassecour . . . a certain day in the year was still kept as a festival to the honour of the . . . patriots and martyrs . . . the morning being given to a solemn Te Deum . . . the evening devoted to spectacles, decorations and illuminations.'

A significant part of the fictional world of the novel is the importance of the Roman Catholic Church. Charlotte, through Lucy, condemns it thoroughly. She sees its influence in the school as pernicious: 'great pains were taken to hide chains with flowers . . . . large sensual indulgence . . . was permitted by way of counterpoise to jealous spiritual restraint'. From this attitude arises Madame Beck's method of ruling her world—by surveillance and espionage. As the secrets of heart and spirit must be confessed, so Madame Beck must know all that passes in the Pensionnat. It is a house where there is no privacy, spiritual or otherwise, and Lucy must retire to the attic to read a letter in private—'a strange house, where no corner was sacred from intrusion'. Even M. Paul has hired a room overlooking the garden from where he can observe his pupils.

Lucy herself, finding her burden of melancholia too great to bear alone, is tempted to the confessional for relief, but her strong, independent, Protestant spirit must fundamentally reject the pressures of a spiritual and physical kind put upon her by Madame Beck and Père Silas.

Part of this world also is the awareness of national feeling and the conflict of nationalities. Lucy's story is primarily enacted in a foreign country, and she must come to terms not only with herself and her fate, but with the 'foreignness' of this environment—with its language, religion, way of life, for Lucy is certainly insular and prejudiced. Nevertheless, the sense of such 'foreignness' and such coming to terms is well presented. Although she may despise the 'continental female', the Roman Catholic religion, and wonder at Madame Beck's method of running her school—'Till noon she haunted the house in her wrapping-gown, shawl and soundless slippers. How would the lady-chief of an English school approve this custom?'—she becomes reconciled to much that is strange—the black stoves, which pleased her little at first, become dark comforters. M. Paul, moreover, disapproves of much that is English in Lucy. In anger he rails against English women, their minds, morals, manners, tall stature, slovenly dress. He refers to that 'conceited boudoir of a first classe with its pretentious book-cases . . . its rubbish of flower-stands . . . its foreign surveillance . . . its new ideas . . . from "la Grande Bretagne": they savoured of island insolence and arrogance'. The resolution of the novel is the resolution of these conflicts on a personal level. M. Paul tells Lucy: 'Remain a Protestant. My little English Puritan, I love Protestantism in you.'

Significantly, this complete if circumscribed society is seen in every case in relation to Lucy's nature and beliefs. She is the unnoticed, anonymous, 'third person in a pink dress and black lace mantle', but she observes, judges, and draws conclusions from all she sees—the sufferings of the king, the intrigues of Ginevra, the nature of the Labassecourienne beauty, the reactions to the painting of Cleopatra. And central to it all is Lucy's own small, personal, but important drama. At the concert, she is amused to witness M. Paul's display of authority and is involved in an encounter with him in the interval—an incident insignificant to all but Lucy. At the Home's party, her exchange of angry words with him is a trivial, unromantic, but extremely important passage set against all the beauty and social success of Paulina.

Villette is not by any means a perfect novel. It has a rambling structure which is less obviously unified than that of *Jane Eyre*. But if we view the novel in terms of its central theme, then the various and varied episodes of Lucy's life can be seen to demonstrate that theme. She is, at each point, observer of the nature and dilemma of others, and aware of her own nature and dilemma at that particular point. Thus, even the Miss Marchmont episode— a period in her life which does not seem to forward anything— might be seen as important in the development of the general theme in that Miss Marchmont gives her 'the originality of her character to study: the steadiness of her virtues . . . the power of her passions to admire; the truth of her feelings to trust'. Miss Marchmont's loss of her lover and her conclusion 'Inscrutable

God, Thy will be done!' is a foreshadowing of Lucy's own fate. The technique of the novel is again, therefore, the technique of parallel example, of symbol and allegory, though the latter is less intrusive than in *Jane Eyre*.

Coincidence and rather schoolgirlish mystery are a fault in the novel's construction, and there is also Charlotte's customary lack of a sense of humour. There is perhaps too much straining after the reader's sympathy for Lucy and her troubles. She is so much the forgotten, suffering, struggling orphan, bravely coming to terms with life. She is also, perhaps, a little too waspish in her views of others. But in spite of such faults, this novel and *Jane Eyre* must be regarded as Charlotte Brontë's highest points of success—one on the melodramatic and religious, the other on the realistic level.

> Cold in the earth, and fifteen wild Decembers
> From those brown hills have melted into spring—
> Faithful indeed is the spirit that remembers
> After such years of change and suffering!

Notably we are made aware of the pressure of life and time upon the living forcing the memory of the dead out of the mind and emotions. So there follows 'the World's tide is bearing me along: /Sterner desires and darker hopes beset me', and existence is 'cherished', 'strengthened', and 'fed', tears are 'checked' and the soul 'weaned from yearning'. The remembrance of the love is still felt and expressed in its force in the final verse:

> And even yet, I dare not let it languish,
> Dare not indulge in Memory's rapturous pain;
> Once drinking deep of that divinest anguish,
> How could I seek the empty world again?

So, out of the conventional situation of the mourner at the tomb, Emily has distilled the essentials of the finality of death, the necessary movement forward into the future of the bereaved, and the urgently felt necessity to suppress the memory of love.

A further example of this kind of development can be seen in the situation, frequently dealt with by her, of the imprisoned captive which develops into the symbolic situation of the spirit's frustration in the imprisonment of the body. This development is most clearly seen in the poem *Julian M. and A. G. Rochelle*. Emily herself perceived that part of this poem might have general recognition as an acknowledged spiritual experience, for she selected part of the poem for publication in the volume of 1846. The poem describes, in familiar terms of melodrama which lead us back to Scott and Byron, Julian M. straying 'in the dungeon crypts':

> Then, God forgive my youth, forgive my careless tongue!
> I scoffed, as the chill chains on the damp flagstones rung;

The captive he mocks has a face 'soft and mild' as 'sculptured marble saint or slumbering, unweaned child'. Julian recognises this captive as a former playmate who expresses, again in conventional terms, the stoicism of the heroic captive in face of hopeless imprisonment: chains cannot long hold her, she has come to accept the disdain and forgetfulness of former friends, yet she is sustained by 'a messenger of Hope'. This is conventional and unmoving enough, but with the mention of this messenger the poem for several stanzas takes on a life and immediacy of its own:

> He comes with western winds, with evening's wandering airs,
> With that clear dusk of heaven that brings the thickest stars;
> Winds take a pensive tone, and stars a tender fire,
> And visions rise and change which kill me with desire—
>
> Desire for nothing known in my maturer years
> When joy grew mad with awe at counting future tears;
> When, if my spirit's sky was full of flashes warm,
> I knew not whence they came, from sun or thunderstorm,
>
> But first a hush of peace, a soundless calm descends;
> The struggle of distress and fierce impatience ends;
> Mute music soothes my breast—unuttered harmony
> That I could never dream till earth was lost to me.
>
> Then dawns the Invisible, the Unseen its truth reveals;
> My outward sense is gone, my inward essence feels—
> Its wings are almost free, its home, its harbour found;
> Measuring the gulf it stoops and dares the final bound!
>
> Oh, dreadful is the check—intense the agony
> When the ear begins to hear and the eye begins to see;
> When the pulse begins to throb, the brain to think again,
> The soul to feel the flesh and the flesh to feel the chain!
>
> Yet I would lose no sting, would wish no torture less;
> The more that anguish racks the earlier it will bless;
> And robed in fires of Hell, or bright with heavenly shine,
> If it but herald Death, the vision is divine.

The working over of this conception of captivity and freedom as it relates to the condition of the soul is perhaps seen at its most skilful in *Riches I hold in light esteem*, a short poem with no sense of requiring the Gondal world behind it. It demonstrates also the simplicity of language and verse-form Emily used:

> Riches I hold in light esteem
> And Love I laugh to scorn
> And lust of Fame was but a dream
> That vanished with the morn—
>
> And if I pray, the only prayer
> That moves my lips for me
> Is—'Leave the heart that now I bear
> And give me liberty.'
>
> Yes, as my swift days near their goal
> 'Tis all that I implore—
> Through life and death, a chainless soul
> With courage to endure!

The Gondal world, where riches, fame and love might be lost and where the qualities of courage, freedom and liberty are demanded, has given rise to a personal statement of the desire for spiritual liberty and endurance.

It is characteristic of her poetry that most of her themes appear first in terms of the conventional literary approach and gradually move to the individual speaking voice of the poet, and this is seen also in her treatment of nature. She begins with the conventional.

> The evening sun, in cloudless shine,
> Had pass'd from summer's heaven divine;
> And dark the shades of twilight grew,
> And stars were in the depth of blue;

and

> For the moors, for the moors where the short grass
> Like velvet beneath us should lie!
> For the moors, for the moors where each high pass
> Rose sunny against the clear sky!

But the poem which reflects her longing for home when she was teaching at Law Hill School concentrates her vision more accurately:

A little and a lone green lane
That opened on a common wide;
A distant, dreamy, dim blue chain
Of mountains circling every side;

A heaven so clear, an earth so calm,
So sweet, so soft, so hushed an air
And, deepening still the dream-like charm,
Wild moor-sheep feeding everywhere—

That was the scene; I knew it well. . . .

The following verse which centres upon two insignificant aspects
of the Yorkshire moors, contrives to conjure up the whole
region for us:

I've seen the purple heather-bell
Look out by many a storm-worn stone;
And oh, I've seen much music swell,
Such wild notes wake these passes lone—

Here, Emily has not only cleared her vision of nature to those
aspects personally known to her but she has also found a way of
making it emotionally strong and pictorially vivid by the use of
a starkly simple language. Such ability to portray the characteristics of the moorland becomes the basis of the ballad-like lament
The linnet in the rocky dells, where the continued activity of nature
is set against the acknowledgment of time's influence on sorrow:

The linnet in the rocky dells,
The moor-lark in the air,
The bee among the heather-bells
That hide my lady fair:

The wild deer browse above her breast;
The wild birds raise their brood;
And they, her smiles of love caressed,
Have left her solitude!

.   .   .

Blow, west wind, by the lonely mound,
And murmur, summer streams,
There is no need of other sound
To sooth my Lady's dreams.

The lightness and simplicity of this poem contrast strongly with her treatment of the similar theme in *Cold in the earth*. Apart from the change of mood in this latter poem, centred on the change to winter, there is a grandeur of movement in the rhythm (though the verse-form remains simple) through the use of repetition, the emphasis initially upon the adjective 'Cold' (a favourite device of Emily's), and the skilful breaking of the natural rhythm.

In these two poems, the natural background, sparsely etched though it may be, begins to take on a symbolic character suited to the mood and subject. But Emily can also make use of aspects of nature for the kind of simple but forceful symbolism which reminds us of Blake, though Emily's symbols lack his suggestion of richness:

> Love is like the wild rose-briar,
> Friendship like the holly-tree—
> The holly is dark when the rose-briar blooms
> But which will bloom most constantly?
>
> The wild rose-briar is sweet in spring,
> Its summer blossoms scent the air;
> Yet wait till winter comes again
> And who will call the wild-briar fair?
>
> Then scorn the silly rose-wreath now
> And deck thee with the holly's sheen,
> And when December blights thy brow
> He still may leave thy garland green.

In spite of her love of nature and her ability to portray concretely aspects of the moorlands she knew, Emily is not a nature poet in the sense that Wordsworth is one. Indeed, the conflict between the pull of nature and the pull of her imaginative world is expressed in poems such as *Shall Earth no more inspire thee*:

> Shall Earth no more inspire thee,
> Thou lonely dreamer now?
> Since passion may not fire thee
> Shall Nature cease to bow?

> Thy mind is ever moving
> In regions dark to thee;
> Recall its useless roving—
> Come back and dwell with me.

And it would seem that certainly through imagination she gained her greatest pleasure:

> Aye, there it is! It wakes tonight
> Sweet thoughts that will not die
> And feeling's fires flash all as bright
> As in the years gone by!
>
> .   .   .
>
> Yes, I could swear that glorious wind
> Has swept that world aside,
> Has dashed its memory from thy mind
> Like foam-bells from the tide—

There is, however, no rejection of nature, for it is not so much specific details of nature that were important to her but the general and eternal characteristics of nature—its movements from spring to winter, cloud to storm, and these are continually present in her poetry, blending often with the emotions drawn from human experience, so that there is no division between human nature and the natural scene. This final unification of man and nature reveals itself in the expressing of human experience in terms of natural phenomena. The second verse quoted above gives us an example of this when the wind is seen as sweeping the mind clear of worldly affairs. In *He comes with western winds*, the spiritual and emotional experience is expressed in terms of the calm of evening—western winds, clear dusk of heaven, the thickest stars. These natural effects merge with human feeling by means of descriptive epithets—'Winds take a *pensive tone*, and stars a *tender fire*' [my italics], and finally we are given a landscape of the mind: 'When, if my spirit's sky was full of flashes warm,/I knew not whence they came, from sun or thunderstorm'. In the poem *Death, that struck when I was most confiding*, the entire experience recalled is envisaged in terms of natural phenomena and the movement of the seasons.

This conception of the unity of nature and human nature accounts for her wide sympathy with all creatures. The poem, *Well, some may hate, and some may scorn*, demonstrates this when the poet finds sympathy for a fallen 'wretch', seeing his sins as being as much part of his individual nature as is the appearance of the wolf part of the wolf's nature, or the cowardice of the leveret part of the leveret's nature (and this recalls *Wuthering Heights* very strongly):

> Do I despise the timid deer
> Because his limbs are fleet with fear?
>
> Or would I mock the wolf's death-howl
> Because his form is gaunt and foul?
> Or hear with joy the leveret's cry
> Because it cannot bravely die?
>
> No! Then above his memory
> Let pity's heart as tender be:
> Say: Earth lie lightly on that breast,
> And, kind Heaven, grant that spirit rest!

Such sympathy does not rule out the strong moral sense of the poems, reflecting a moral consciousness which is in no way narrow, but is yet Christian and stoic. Courage, endurance and freedom are the qualities most desired, and Emily's most moving expression of her belief in a brave independent soul which is part of God and his universe appears in this poem:

> No coward soul is mine
> No trembler in the world's storm-troubled sphere
> I see Heaven's glories shine
> And Faith shines equal arming me from Fear.
>
> O God within my breast
> Almighty ever-present Deity
> Life, that in me hast rest
> As I Undying Life, have power in Thee.

Set against this, we have her perception of the injustices of this world and the need of a brave soul to look upon these and acknowledge its helplessness to change them:

There was a time when my cheek burned
To give such scornful fiends the lie;
Ungoverned nature madly spurned
The law that bade it not defy.
O in the days of ardent youth
I would have given my life for truth.

For truth, for right, for liberty,
I would have gladly, freely died;
And now I calmly hear and see
The vain man smile, the fool deride;
Though not because my heart is tame,
Though not for fear, though not for shame.

My soul still chafes at every tone
Of selfish and self-blinded error;
My breast still braves the world alone,
Steeled as it ever was to terror;
Only I know, however I frown,
The same world will go rolling on.

In spite of the kind of themes she dealt with, Emily's poetry is
most noticeable for, and derives much of its strength and originality from, the sense it gives of the lonely, isolated inquiry of a
single soul, with the resulting sense of strong independence and
individualism, characteristics which again we find in her novel.
This kind of attitude is no doubt in part responsible for the form
which some poems take, that of the inquiry, as in *Shall Earth
no more inspire thee* and *Aye, there it is! It wakes tonight.* It is also
responsible for the high place given in her work to the delights
of the imagination and of the freedom provided by the mystic
experience.

She is not an originator or innovator either in thought or
technique. The strength of her work and its originality derive
from the simplicity of language and symbol and her use of
traditional and unobtrusive verse-forms, particularly those
reminiscent of the ballad and the 18th-century hymn. These
provide, in her best poems, a firm vehicle for ideas which, though
not original, are notable for the intensity with which they are
held.

It has been pointed out by commentators that certain aspects of *Wuthering Heights* are foreshadowed in the poems. The dark stranger with long black hair and eyes with a basilisk charm, who calls at a peasant's house, reminds us of Heathcliff. And the verse:

> Though earth and moon were gone,
> And suns and universes cease to be,
> And thou wert left alone,
> Every existence would exist in thee . . .

recalls Catherine's claim that if 'all else perished and *he* [Heathcliff] remained, I should still continue to be . . .' Heathcliff might have said of himself:

> And yet, for all her hate, each parting glance would tell
> A stronger passion breathed, burned in this last farewell.
> Unconquered in my soul the Tyrant rules me still—
> *Life* bows to my control, but *love* I cannot kill.

The poem beginning 'The soft unclouded blue of air', which describes an 'iron man' with 'stern and swarthy brow', is surely an early reflection of Heathcliff's nature and predicament. But it is primarily in the working over of her chosen themes of the soul's freedom, the loss of a loved one, the sense of exile from a heaven (earthly or otherwise), the conception of the soul's restless desire for another condition, the close relationship between man and nature, that the poetry would seem to have been preparation for the novel.

The poem which has been attributed to Charlotte, but which is surely Emily's, is characteristic of her in its spirit of independence, its balancing of imagination and nature. And the final acknowledgment of the possible importance of this earth is perhaps a sign of her turning towards the life of the moors for the appropriate setting of those Gondalian themes which appear in *Wuthering Heights*.

> Often rebuked, yet always back returning
> To those first feelings that were born with me,

And leaving busy chase of wealth and learning
    For idle dreams of things which cannot be:

To-day, I will seek not the shadowy region;
    Its unsustaining vastness waxes drear;
And visions rising, legion after legion,
    Bring the unreal world too strangely near.

I'll walk, but not in old heroic traces,
    And not in paths of high morality,
And not among the half-distinguished faces,
    The clouded forms of long-past history.

I'll walk where my own nature would be leading:
    It vexes me to choose another guide:
Where the gray flocks in ferny glens are feeding;
    Where the wild wind blows on the mountain side.

What have those lonely mountains worth revealing?
    More glory and more grief than I can tell:
The earth that wakes *one* human heart to feeling
    Can centre both the world of Heaven and Hell.

8

Wuthering Heights—I

'Whether it is right or advisable to create beings like Heathcliff, I do not know: I scarcely think it is,' wrote Charlotte Brontë doubtfully in her 1850 Preface to Emily Brontë's *Wuthering Heights*. The terms 'right' and 'advisable' are moral terms which we would hardly think of applying to Emily's creation of Heathcliff, though we might judge morally of Heathcliff as a man in the fictional context of the novel. Charlotte went on to justify the creation in terms of the artist's necessity to create what he must: 'Be the work grim or glorious, dread or divine, you have little choice left but quiescent adoption.'

Charlotte, in her Preface, was attempting to answer the charges that reviewers had laid against her sister's novel, for *Wuthering Heights* received much criticism. The setting in itself —the then unknown Yorkshire moors, with the rough manners and unintelligible dialect—was partly responsible for the unfavourable reception. The novel was condemned as being 'coarse in language and coarse in conception'; it was 'unquestionably and irremediably monstrous' containing 'physical acts of cruelty . . . which true taste rejects'; it had 'a moral taint' about it; it was 'the extraordinary and feverish romance'; and the only moral to be found in it was to show 'what Satan could do with the law of Entail'.

We can move from such criticism to that of our own century, where the emphasis has changed from a consideration of the novel as degrading, to a feeling that it is the work of a mystic and a genius: 'Her great characters exist in virtue of the reality of their attitude to the universe,' they are revealed 'against the huge landscape of the cosmic scheme'; and, seeing Emily as drawn towards 'storm' and 'calm', the first part of the novel examines the values of the storm, the second, the nature of the calm. Whereas Charlotte described Nelly Dean as 'a specimen of true benevolence and homely fidelity', a modern critic sees her as the villain of the piece, taking Nelly's own words as his text: 'I seated myself in a chair, and rocked, to and fro, passing harsh judgment on my many derelictions of duty; from which, it struck me then, all the misfortunes of all my employers sprang . . . I thought Heathcliff himself less guilty than I.'

Such a range of reactions demonstrates at any rate the power of the book and its complexity. Certainly it is the most finished of all the Brontë novels in its more complete artistic vision and in its superior fictional technique. Emily is able to view her material more objectively than Charlotte, and she never descends to the pedestrianism of Anne. She avoids the mistakes of wrong emphasis and intrusive material that the other two were guilty of. Most surprising, perhaps, is the fact that whereas, in Charlotte's novels, we can trace a developing vision and skill, Emily appears to have produced a finished masterpiece without any early stages of trial and error.

AN INCREDIBLE TALE

Heathcliff, an orphan from the slums of Liverpool, is brought home to Wuthering Heights by its owner, Mr. Earnshaw, who makes the boy one of the family. His son, Hindley, develops an undying hatred for Heathcliff, his daughter, Cathy, an undying love. In his turn, Heathcliff hates Hindley and loves Cathy.

After the death of Mr. Earnshaw, Hindley degrades Heathcliff to the level of a farm-worker, and Cathy, though she loves him, realises that she cannot marry him. She agrees to marry instead Edgar Linton, son of the Linton family of Thrushcross Grange. Heathcliff, hearing of this, runs away.

He returns after three years, wealthy and a gentleman, and determined to avenge himself on the two families. Cathy is now married and living at the Grange with Edgar and his sister Isabella and Nelly Dean, formerly the servant at the Heights. Hindley, on the death of his wife Frances, has turned to drinking and gambling. Heathcliff stays with him, corrupting him further and degrading his small son, Hareton.

As a result of Heathcliff's return, Cathy quarrels with Edgar and becomes ill. Heathcliff elopes with Isabella. Cathy dies after giving birth to the young Catherine Linton; Isabella escapes from the Heights and leaves the area, eventually giving birth to a son, Linton Heathcliff; and Hindley Earnshaw dies, leaving his property and his son in Heathcliff's hands.

After a period of twelve years, Isabella dies, and Heathcliff claims his son. Still later, he forces Catherine Linton to marry Linton Heathcliff, who dies shortly afterwards. Hareton, the younger Catherine and Nelly Dean are all living at the Heights, when Heathcliff dies, and the marriage of Hareton and Catherine is then planned.

In many ways this story of a man's two passions of love and hatred is an incredible one. At the same time it is a simple tale in its outlines, and in many other aspects. Its incredibilities and its simplicities would seem, in part, to come from the influence of the folk-tale, the ballad, Gothic novels of horror, Byron and Scott.

The story begins in folk-tale fashion with a father setting out on a journey and asking his children what they would like him to bring back as presents. The usurping of a higher position by a menial, with the usurped person disguised as a menial, is a folk-tale theme.

The presentation of character and the development of relationships is generally not of the kind we expect in a novel. We have to take for granted that Heathcliff and Catherine form their strong relationship in childhood, that Edgar Linton is captivated by her, that Isabella should fall equally suddenly in love with Heathcliff, that the second Catherine should be attracted to Hareton. Whereas George Eliot or Jane Austen, or Charlotte Brontë herself, would each in her different way show such attractions developing from first meeting to subsequent relationships, into love, and analyse and reveal the reasons for such relationships, in *Wuthering Heights* we are told it was so, it happened thus, without explanation or analysis. Catherine 'gained the admiration of

Isabella, and the heart and soul of her brother'; 'Miss Cathy and [Heathcliff] were now very thick'; 'Isabella Linton evinced a sudden and irresistible attraction towards the tolerated guest.' Heathcliff himself, with his mysterious origin and arrival at the Heights, is a character of folk-tale and ballad, and in his career there is much of the Byronic hero, the demon lover, and the villain of the Gothic novel whose villainy could not be overcome. Macaulay described the typical Byronic hero as 'A man proud, moody, cynical, with defiance on his brow, and misery in his heart, a scorner of his kind, implacable in revenge, yet capable of deep and strong affection.' The Gothic influence is also apparent at the Heights with its isolation, mystery and old retainers. Indeed, the convention of the Gothic novel which involved the arrival of a stranger at a mysterious mansion is repeated several times in the novel—with Lockwood, Isabella and the younger Catherine. And the tradition of imprisonment in such places is apparent in the case of Isabella, Catherine, and Linton Heathcliff.

The violence and sadism which exists in the novel and yet evokes no reaction from outside forces of law and order, and which is largely accepted by the characters involved, is a further extravagance. Even allowing for the early dating of the action— the 1770s to 1801—and the isolated setting, such a concentration of violence cannot be accepted easily. Hindley tries to force the carving-knife between Nelly's teeth and drops Hareton over the bannister; Heathcliff hangs Isabella's dog, kicks and tramples on Hindley and dashes his head against the flags, throws a dinner knife at Isabella; Hareton hangs puppies from a kitchen chair. And the violence extends into the imagery of the novel—'The tyrant grinds down his slaves'; fingers are 'instruments that will do execution'; Heathcliff will crush Isabella 'like a sparrow's egg'.

In face of such violence and sadism, one feels inclined to quote Henry Tilney's words to Catherine Morland in *Northanger Abbey*, a novel which was being written during the years 1800–1810: 'Remember the country and the age in which we live. Remember that we are English; that we are Christians . . . does our education prepare us for such atrocities? Do our laws connive at them?'

And beneath the violence and incredible action lies a pattern of human relationships which is unrealistic in its very symmetry. Two sets of parents—the Earnshaws and the Lintons—have each two offspring, each pair made up of a son and a daughter. A son in one case (Hindley Earnshaw) marries an outsider (Frances); a daughter (Isabella Linton) in the other case marries Heathcliff. The remaining children (Catherine Earnshaw and Edgar Linton) marry and unite the families. Of these three marriages are born three children—Hareton Earnshaw, Catherine Linton, and Linton Heathcliff. Catherine marries first one son, Linton, and then the other, Hareton, by which time all the other members of the two families are dead, and the families are narrowed down to this pair.

This strange formality is seen in the constant interchanging of the family names, particularly in the case of the two Catherines. Catherine Earnshaw writes her name three times—as Catherine Earnshaw, her maiden name, as Catherine Heathcliff, the name she would like to have, as Catherine Linton, her married name. Her daughter starts as Catherine Linton, by a first marriage becomes Catherine Heathcliff, and by a second marriage, Catherine Earnshaw, so reversing the process. A similar formally controlled movement is seen in the extension of Heathcliff's power over the two houses and their heirs and its recession, leaving the heirs in possession of their inheritance again.

Such formality, while it is unrealistic, does provide a feeling of strength and inevitability. Beneath the incredibly wild and the incredibly formal elements of the novel, we have a world which is based on actuality—legal, temporal, and geographical—indicating careful planning by the author.

BASIC ACTUALITY

Heathcliff's story is plotted in time from his arrival at the Heights in the summer of 1776 to his death in May 1802. It is possible from the evidence within the novel to fix almost all the events in terms of dating, thus suggesting a very conscious author, not a wild, romantic one.

Nelly Dean's narrative covers the years 1776 to 1802, and one wonders why Emily set the novel so far back. Closer examination of these years shows that the action of the novel centres in short bursts covering a briefer period of this longer stretch. For example, from 1777 (Hindley's return to the Heights) to 1780 (Heathcliff runs away), there are three years of intensive action and emotion which result from Hindley's treatment of Heathcliff and the effect of the Linton influence upon Cathy. The second 'packed' period of time is from September 1783 (Heathcliff's return) to March 1784 when Isabella escapes from the Heights. The third period is from March 1800 to November 1800—eight months which see the beginning of the Cathy–Linton relationship; March 1801 to October 1801, sees the completion of Heathcliff's plans.

Within each of these periods, we are aware of advance and recession; and of unimportant periods of time being covered in a few sentences: 'Edgar Linton . . . believed himself the happiest man alive on the day he led her to Gimmerton chapel, three years subsequent to his father's death.' 'The twelve years . . . following that dismal period, were the happiest of my life . . .' And each period ends on a climax of pain and passion—Heathcliff's departure and Cathy's distress; Cathy's death and Isabella's escape; Edgar's severing of Linton and Cathy's relationship; Linton's death and Cathy's illness and defeat. Each, in ending on such a climax, allows for a period of calm and regrowth before another assault. The final period, with its movement to Heathcliff's death and the growing love of Cathy and Hareton, reverses the process and allows for a final movement into calmness.

But Nelly's narrative is enclosed within the frame of Lockwood's narrative, and this is equally carefully planned in terms of time and season. Lockwood's experience of the situation begins in late November or early December 1801 when he pays his first two visits to the Heights as tenant of the Grange. There follows the period of his illness during which he hears Nelly's story, and, in late January 1802, he visits the Heights again to tell Heathcliff he is leaving the area. Thus, his first stay at the Grange covers a period of about five weeks and brings Nelly's story up to October

1801 when Cathy went to live at the Heights just before Lockwood became tenant of the Grange.

Lockwood returns to the Grange in September 1802, again visits the Heights, and hears the end of the story—the events leading to Heathcliff's death in May 1802.

Within this larger time scheme is the movement of the seasons which Nelly chronicles with detail and atmosphere—Christmas at the Heights, summer on the moors, wet autumns, and bitter winters. And in the forefront, in the present time, we have the period of winter storms and illness moving to the mild harvest period of September.

Human life is seen also within this period moving continually from birth to death. Thus Hareton, Cathy and Linton are born, Mr. Earnshaw ages and sickens, Heathcliff broadens and puts on weight, Nelly becomes stout.

Geographically also, the fictional area of the novel is carefully planned. Apart from the evocation of the Yorkshire moors and their isolation, the appropriate farming activities, and the reference to the near-by coal, there is the strong dialect of Joseph, the farming custom of living in the 'house', the Methodist influence, the doctor, the curate, the lawyer. More precisely, we know it is four miles from Thrushcross to the Heights, and a mile and a half further on to Penistone Crag.

In terms of the legal background to the property in the novel, Emily Brontë is also accurate, and Heathcliff's actions depend upon it. He obtains Wuthering Heights by becoming Hindley's mortgagee. Thrushcross Grange is entailed to Edgar's sons, but not to his daughters, therefore, since he has no heir, the property goes next to Mr. Linton's daughter, Isabella, and is entailed to her son, Linton. Heathcliff wants Catherine married to Linton before he dies to ensure that there can be no dispute over his claim to the Grange and to her personal property.

But the emotional fidelity comes from brief touches of the normal episodes and incidents of life, which are given by Emily Brontë with a strong, controlled, emotive quality. They reflect the essentials of human life into the stormy and metaphysical world of the passions. The news of Hareton's birth brought to

Nelly while she is working in the fields: '. . . the girl that usually brought our breakfasts came running an hour too soon, across the meadow and up the lane, calling me as she ran. "Oh, such a grand bairn!" she panted out'; Nelly in the living room at the Heights, with the house prepared for Christmas; Cathy sitting by the window and saying, 'Oh! I'm tired—I'm *stalled*, Hareton!'

However exaggerated Heathcliff and his passions and actions may appear to be, therefore, there is nothing improbable basically in the story and setting, which is firmly grounded in social, legal, and family observances and events.

A CUCKOO'S HISTORY

Nelly Dean specifically calls her story—which is fundamentally the story of Heathcliff—a cuckoo's history. Heathcliff is thus, from the beginning, identified by Nelly with a natural occurrence. The cuckoo lays its egg in the nest of another bird, and the young cuckoo, once hatched, eventually ejects the other young birds, absorbs the whole attention of the parent birds, and takes over the nest. If we take the birds and their nest as the type of home and family life, we can see the nature of Heathcliff's part in the history of the Earnshaw family as that of the usurper. We are, therefore, involved from the beginning in the traditional conceptions of family relationships, heritage, and customs accepted by society.

Heathcliff immediately begins to reverse the customs of the Earnshaw family. Although we are given no picture of the family life before his arrival, the indications are of a normal household, yet Heathcliff at once involves the inhabitants of the house in acts of inhospitality and hatred. Nelly leaves him on the landing to sleep, the young Catherine spits at him. Later we find him coming between Hindley, the son of the house, and his father.

His revenge is also a cuckoo's action, disrupting the two households with which he is associated, appropriating heritages, bringing family dissension, ultimately laying claim to both heirs and their properties. This is not only an extension of the inhospitable treatment he received as a child in both houses, it is a revenge on the degradation in social terms which he suffered, and on the taking of Cathy from him through the influence of society and its claims.

Following Mr. Earnshaw's death, Heathcliff is relegated to the position of a servant by Hindley. He is deprived of education, made to work on the farm, and treated to beatings and separation from Catherine. But such treatment, although it degrades him in mind and appearance, does not affect his close relationship with Catherine. This is severed only by her contact with the comfort and customs of society through the Linton family. It is after her return from the Grange that Catherine becomes aware of the gap between herself and Heathcliff. He is dirty, uncouth, and has nothing to say for himself. As a result, Catherine is first involved in the dilemma which is to be their mutual undoing.

Edgar Linton proposes marriage and Cathy accepts because he is rich, handsome and young, and because, she says, she loves him. Though she knows she is wrong in marrying him, she will not face up to the inevitable separation from Heathcliff. To marry Heathcliff, however, would degrade her. It would involve her perpetually in the world the Heights has become.

In this contest, Heathcliff's manner of return is significant. He returns with, superficially, all those qualities which he would have required for Cathy to marry him—wealth, the appearance and manners of a gentleman: 'his manner was even dignified'. But a 'half-civilised ferocity lurked yet in the depressed brows', and neither Nelly nor Cathy are deceived. They recognise that the same nature exists, and Cathy also recognises that 'avarice is growing with him a besetting sin'.

HEATHCLIFF'S REVENGE

Heathcliff makes no secret to Catherine of his intention to revenge himself, and he begins his revenge with plans for taking over the property and wealth of both the Earnshaw and Linton families. When the quarrel over Isabella begins, we do not hear the whole of it, but we do know that, to some extent, he and Cathy are quarrelling over the disposition of the Linton wealth. He threatens, by marrying Isabella, to stand Catherine aside.

His revenge will also be in terms of social degradation, as well as in the taking over of property. So Isabella is degraded. When Nelly visits her after her marriage: '... she already partook of the pervading spirit of neglect which encompassed her. Her pretty face was wan and listless; her hair uncurled ... So much had circumstances altered their positions, that he [Heathcliff] would certainly have struck a stranger as a born and bred gentleman, and his wife a thorough little slattern!' Hareton 'was reduced to a state of complete dependence on his father's inveterate enemy; and lives in his own house as a servant'.

But, just as Heathcliff considers that his own nature was perverted by his rejection, so he revenges himself in terms of a similar perversion of others. His means of revenge come through his perception of the nature of others—of Isabella's love for him, of the young Cathy's love for Linton. He destroys Hindley by encouraging his vices of drinking and gambling, he attempts to destroy the lovable nature of the young Cathy: 'the only sentiment they [her eyes] evinced hovered between scorn and a kind of desperation, singularly unnatural to be detected there'. The pleasure he takes in what he has done to Hareton derives not only from the degradation of the heir to the Heights and the fact that he is a servant on what was his own property, but from the fact that he perceives that Hareton has a fine nature which he has destroyed:

> If he were a born fool I should not enjoy it half so much. But he's no fool; and I can sympathise with all his feelings, having felt them myself ... And he'll never be able to emerge from his bathos of coarseness and ignorance. I've got him faster than his scoundrel of a father secured me, and lower; for he takes a pride in his brutishness.
>
> Chapter XXI

And just as the person he loved most was taken from him, so Heathcliff inflicts pain by severing those human relationships which involve love. Edgar Linton loses sister, wife, and daughter through his machinations.

Heathcliff's revenge becomes, eventually, not so much the work of a man but of a superhuman force for evil. Certainly in its tenacity, ruthlessness and determination, it is this. He has, as he says, got 'levers and mattocks to demolish the two houses'—this is his intention. But it goes beyond this. 'The more the worms writhe, the more I yearn to crush out their entrails! It is a moral teething.' The stifling of pity and all human emotion and response on his part is a 'moral teething' in terms of taking him beyond all moral concerns into an amoral world of ruthless hatred. To Nelly he comments on his wife:

> 'She degenerates into a mere slut . . . It was a marvellous effort of perspicacity to discover that I did not love her . . . Now, was it not the depth of absurdity—of genuine idiocy, for that pitiful, slavish, mean-minded brach to dream that I could love her? Tell your master, Nelly, that I never, in all my life, met with such an abject thing as she is. She even disgraces the name of Linton; and I've sometimes relented, from pure lack of invention, in my experiments on what she could endure, and still creep shamefully cringing back. But tell him, also, to set his fraternal and magisterial heart at ease, that I keep strictly within the limits of the law.'   Chapter XIV

His attitude and behaviour to his own son reaches the climax of unnaturalness. Linton is 'it' to him from the first: 'God! what a beauty! What a lovely, charming thing . . . Haven't they reared it on snails and sour milk, Nelly?' Linton is seen only as a further instrument of his revenge. He terrorises the dying boy into carrying out his wishes and bringing Cathy to the house. Once his plans for their marriage are complete, he is no longer concerned with what becomes of him: '. . . never let me hear a word more about him! None here care what becomes of him; if you do, act the nurse; if you do not, lock him up and leave him.'

THE COMMON SYMPATHIES OF HUMAN NATURE

Heathcliff's evil and violent nature and the success with which he carries out his revenge transform him eventually from a credible being into a fiend. In his ability to paralyse anything good and pervert the most ordinary and decent nature, there is something beyond the natural, even though he works within the bounds of law, his insight into the nature of others, and his own brute strength. In many ways, Heathcliff is a figure of folk-tale —an ogre in his castle with the ability to work magic. It is not surprising that Isabella asks, 'Is Mr. Heathcliff a man? If so, is he mad? And if not, is he a devil?' And at the same time she recognises the effect of Heathcliff's influence: 'How did you contrive to preserve the common sympathies of human nature when you resided here? I cannot recognise any sentiment which those around share with me.' It is the 'common sympathies of human nature' which Heathcliff succeeds in drying up. Zillah, fully aware that Heathcliff's son Linton is dying, does nothing to get a doctor: 'I never dare disobey him, Mrs. Dean, and though I thought it wrong that [Dr.] Kenneth should not be sent for, it was no concern of mine . . . Once or twice . . . I've seen her [Linton's wife] sitting crying, on the stairs' top; and then I've shut myself in, quick, for fear of being moved to interfere. I did pity her then, I'm sure: still I didn't want to lose my place, you know.'

On no occasion does anyone seem able to do anything to put matters right. Good is passive in face of evil. The curate is driven away from the Heights, Linton is prevented from helping Hareton by the threat that if Hareton is reclaimed, Heathcliff will demand his son. Heathcliff's presence is seen to be a visitation of the devil, not only through the comments of other characters upon him, but particularly through Nelly's view of him:

> His visits were a continual nightmare to me; and, I suspected, to my master also. His abode at the Heights was an oppression past explaining. I felt that God had forsaken the stray sheep there to its own wicked wanderings, and an evil beast prowled between it and the fold, waiting his time to spring and destroy.   Chapter X

CATHERINE EARNSHAW

Catherine Earnshaw's tragedy was that she was faced with an impossible choice—between Heathcliff who, though degraded, is more herself than she is, and Edgar Linton who stands for the wealthy, cultivated, but much tamer and more restricted existence. In making the decision to marry Edgar, she did not realise fully that it meant cutting herself off not only from Heathcliff, but from the wildness and freedom she had enjoyed as a child. Her true nature is wild and rough and passionate, but, in face of the 'invariable courtesy' she experiences at the Grange, she conceals her true nature, and 'adopts a double character'. Thus, she is ladylike with the Lintons, but reverts to her natural self at the Heights. It is this natural self which Linton glimpses when she nips Nelly, shakes Hareton, and slaps Linton himself, so that he says to her, 'You've made me afraid and ashamed of you.'

The scene of her delirium is very important. Heathcliff's return has aroused that true nature which the life at Thrushcross has allowed to lie buried. Now she finds herself between the two men—Heathcliff, already changed and growing insubordinate to her will, and Edgar too calm and controlled to appreciate her passionate nature. First, the thought of Edgar's calmness in face of her suffering torments her to the idea of death. Through her own action she has chosen the controlled, but wealthy man. Now she finds herself in what she thinks of as a hostile environment—Edgar, Isabella, Nelly, all disliking or fearing her, wanting her out of the way so that things can return to normal. Then, reverting to Heathcliff, she remembers how he set a trap over a lapwing's nest so that the parent could not feed its young—'we saw its nest in the winter, full of little skeletons'. In her delirium, she sees clearly what Heathcliff is—the unnatural being who comes between parent and child, who disrupts the course of nature with deliberate and senseless cruelty. But 'I made him promise he'd never shoot a lapwing after that'. This reflects her former control over Heathcliff. But a moment later, she doubts that control—'Did he shoot my lapwings, Nelly?' Then she sees Nelly as an old witch who wants to cause mischief—which in part she does. Finally, she imagines herself removed from the Heights as a child, without any introductory process, and set down into the Grange, and envisages her misery. This is the way she would have felt had she been taken from Wuthering Heights and Heathcliff as a child, and this is, fundamentally, the source of her unhappiness now. For this reason, she wants to return to the Heights and childhood—the period of her freedom and happiness. For this reason also, she sees her only means of being reunited with Heathcliff as being through death.

Catherine's passionate nature, frustrated, destroys itself, whereas Heathcliff's turns outwards and destroys others, but is itself ultimately worn out: 'Nelly, there is a strange change approaching: I'm in its shadow . . .'

CONTRAST OF THE TWO HOUSES

The concern with social position and manners, with the possession and inheritance of property, with civilisation and brutality, extends also to the physical background of the two houses. The Heights is associated with the violence, hatred and degradation of human nature, the Grange with more civilising, less passionate emotions, with softer manners, the preservation of law, order, accepted religion. But it implies also a weakening and a making petty of human nature and emotion, and it is open to corruption by the advent of stronger, uncontrolled barbarism of hatred and revenge.

It is interesting to notice that when Heathcliff's revenge has been completed, the Grange is left abandoned to a tenant or to vacancy. But when his revenge at length destroys him, it is the Heights that is to be shut up and the Grange which is to be the centre of society again.

Wuthering Heights

The first chapters establish the nature of the house itself. The pattern of inhospitality, of the house being difficult of ingress and equally difficult of egress, of containing little comfort beyond the living room, and of being, upstairs, a maze of inhospitable and abandoned rooms and passages in which a stranger may easily wander discomforted, is repeated again and again.

The young Heathcliff is left by Nelly Dean on the landing when the children refuse to have him with them, and he 'crept to Mr. Earnshaw's door' and slept on the floor outside. Heathcliff and Catherine as children are forced into cold corners, freezing attics, or out on the moors. Isabella Linton, coming there after her marriage, can find no room in which to eat her supper or sleep. Cathy Linton, visiting the house as a young girl, is refused attention by Hareton and Zillah, and when she goes there as Linton's wife is left in the cold bedroom to nurse him till he dies, and then left alone in her illness until she can bear the cold no longer. It is a house where the gates and doors are barred, and the windows small, where Cathy and Nelly are imprisoned. Frequently there is a feeling of danger even in crossing its threshold. And either the inmates or the weather may prevent one leaving again.

So, from Heathcliff's arrival, we have a house which in spite of its apparent normality as a farmhouse with physical comfort and working areas, is actually abnormally inhospitable, with a perverse, forbidding atmosphere, and a haunted room. Even Catherine's attempt at repaying hospitality by inviting the Lintons to dinner at Christmas-time is marred by the immediate quarrel between Heathcliff and Linton. It is the setting for physical and mental violence and cruelty, which begins with Heathcliff and Hindley as children fighting over the ponies, and goes on to Hindley being trampled beneath Heathcliff's feet, and the young Cathy's shocking and lonely vigil with her dying husband.

Only at the end of the story, with Heathcliff's power lessening, does normality begin to return in Cathy's attempt at a garden, Nelly's parlour, the taking up of normal occupations and relationships.

Thrushcross Grange

The Grange is not described in such detail as the Heights. The only extensive description of it is given by Heathcliff when he describes how Cathy and himself watch the young Lintons through the drawing-room window: ' . . . a splendid place carpeted with crimson, and crimson-covered chairs and tables, and a pure white ceiling, bordered by gold, a shower of glass-drops hanging in silver chains from the centre, and shimmering with little soft tapers.' We know that there is a library at the Grange and an extensive park. But if the physical details are left vague, the moral and human ambience is made clear. Initially, when old Mr. and Mrs. Linton are alive, it is the centre of civilised and ordered living and moral standards, in spite of the spoilt pettiness and weakliness of the two Linton children:

> And then Mr. Linton . . . paid us a visit himself on the morrow; and read the young master such a lecture on the road he guided his family, that he was stirred to look about him, in earnest . . . Mrs. Earnshaw undertook to keep her sister-in-law in due restraint when she returned home . . .   Chapter VI

Its influence is so strong, that Cathy is transformed—superficially at least—after five weeks in the house, returning not a rough, wild creature but 'a very dignified person, with brown ringlets falling from the cover of a feathered beaver, and a long cloth habit, which she was obliged to hold up with both hands that she might sail in'.

But the Grange, just as it is civilising, is also weakening in its influence, and it has no power against intruders as has the Heights. Heathcliff gains access easily, and brings dissension in a short time, little Linton Heathcliff cannot be kept there for long, Cathy escapes from it whenever she wishes, and eventually Heathcliff is able to walk in, its undisputed master. Edgar Linton is a magistrate and to some extent the house is the seat of law and order, there is regular church attendance on the part of its inmates, but neither law nor religion is proof against the force that emanates from Heathcliff. He can corrupt lawyers, and use the Sabbath as excuse to visit the dying Catherine. Isabella, when she comes to run away from her husband, will not linger at the Grange, for she feels no safety there from Heathcliff. There is kindness, gentleness, and love among its inmates, but no emotion and no tie is strong enough to be proof against the outside world.

9

Wuthering Heights—II

One of the difficulties in coming to terms with *Wuthering Heights* on any level save that of a wild and Gothic and gripping tale of love and revenge, is the lack of any final commentary on the action as a whole. We are provided with plenty of incidental commentary of a moral or philosophical nature, or of a religious nature, by Lockwood, Nelly Dean and Joseph, but none of their comments will stand as final commentary. This is partly due to the narrative technique, which removes the author entirely from the scene; but there was nothing to stop Emily Brontë making Nelly Dean the one who could give the comment, or Lockwood, for that matter. Yet while Nelly's comments are often sound, we frequently feel that because she is conventional and limited, she cannot see the action in perspective.

The most obtrusive impression that emerges is the fiend-like, Satanic influence of Heathcliff, yet we do not feel that it was Emily Brontë's sole intention to supply us with such a purely grotesque eruption into the normal world, as of a figure from hell.

The need to find a more comprehensive interpretation is seen in the very early reviews: 'We are not disposed to ascribe any particular intention to the author in drawing the character of Heathcliff, nor can we perceive any very obvious moral in the story.' But we can observe a possible authorial intention in the commentary of the action of the novel upon itself. To begin with, we can see that the effect of Heathcliff's action is an upsetting and disregarding of all established modes of thought and conduct— on the level of manners, class convention and religion.

MANNERS

On the level of manners, or sophisticated social observance, commentary is centred mainly round Lockwood. Lockwood is the sophisticated, conceited town-dweller, afraid of emotional involvement in life, who, although uncomprehending of the real situation at the Heights, is one of the most disturbed by it. The house has a powerful effect upon him. He is made a fool of by the treatment he receives there, but he also is susceptible to its influences, as his dreams show, even to the extent of acting out (through fear) the most cruel act in the cruel world of the Heights: 'As it spoke, I discerned, obscurely, a child's face looking through the window. Terror made me cruel; and, finding it useless to attempt shaking the creature off, I pulled its wrist on to the broken pane, and rubbed it to and fro till the blood ran down and soaked the bedclothes: still it wailed, "Let me in!"'

For Lockwood, his stay in the area involves a shattering both of his romantic and his conventional social expectations of life. Beginning with the pleasure of discovering for himself such a misanthropist's Heaven, after four weeks he is disenchanted with the bleak winds and bitter northern skies and the dearth of human physiognomy. The young Catherine's attitude to him is similarly a blow to his self-esteem. He cannot understand why she has not fallen in love with him—an interesting stranger—but at the same time is rather glad she hasn't.

His visits to the Heights are a constant confrontation between what he expects in terms of conventional social behaviour and the treatment he receives.

His first visit gives us a description of the house's exterior and interior—at least of the living-room with its sanded floor and dresser. But Lockwood's expectations of normal hospitality are upset by the attack of the dogs upon him. He still thinks in conventional terms, however, of Joseph as 'the whole establishment of domestics' and Heathcliff as not wanting to lose a good tenant.

His second visit discloses to him how mistaken he has been. Seeing 'the missus', he bows, waiting to be asked to take a seat. Cathy's response is to remain silent and to look at him. An attempt to reach down the tea cannister for Catherine is snapped off with 'I don't want your help', and when he cannot admit that he has been asked to tea, she refuses to make any at all. His reaction at the tea table is again conventional: 'I thought, if I had caused the cloud, it was my duty to make an effort to dispel it. They could not every day sit so grim and taciturn . . .' But his attempts at conversation only bring him up against the odd relationships there—Cathy is not Heathcliff's wife, nor is she Hareton's. He begins to realise the truth of the Heights: 'The dismal spiritual atmosphere overcame, and more than neutralised the glowing physical comforts around me.' Attacked by the dogs, he is eventually shown to a bedroom by the servant who does not know why her master has 'an odd notion about the chamber' she is to put him in. His sleep is disturbed by the dream and the ghost, and he is finally startled by Heathcliff's passionate address to it: 'Come in! come in! . . . Cathy, do come.' The yard being haunted by dogs, the living-room by Juno, Lockwood is forced to the kitchen.

On this level of expectation Nelly thinks that by washing and tidying Heathcliff, making him socially presentable, she can break through all the barriers round him; Edgar Linton attempts to put Heathcliff's return on this level: 'Mrs. Linton, recalling old times, would have me give you a cordial reception; and, of course, I am gratified when anything occurs to please her.' Significantly, such expectations are shattered. The characters pay no more heed to them than to religious beliefs. They are constantly being reversed. Hot apple sauce is thrown, there is nipping and scratching and tormenting on social occasions, host and guest are involved in physical blows.

CONVENTIONAL RELIGION AND MORALITY

Nelly being the main narrator and most intimate observer of the action, her conventional religious and moral beliefs permeate the story, yet we feel they are inadequate on account of her own limited perception. Healthy, placid, unstirred by strong emotion and therefore incapable of appreciating it, she can be a deceptive witness though an accurate and honest reporter. Hers is a moral comprehension of a limited kind, depending upon moral and religious clichés which are, nevertheless, sound and sensible. They are adequate for her own existence, but inadequate in face of Heathcliff and Catherine.

Questioned by Catherine as to whether she has done right in promising to marry Edgar Linton, Nelly responds: 'You have pledged your word, and cannot retract.' Listening to Isabella's story of her experiences with Heathcliff, she comments, 'If God afflict your enemies, surely that ought to suffice you' and '. . . laughter is sadly out of place under this roof, and in your condition!'

At the climax of Heathcliff's life, Nelly can only be concerned that he should read his Bible, and wonder whether his failure of appetite might be viewed as an attempt at suicide, and what is to be put on his gravestone since he has only one name and no known date of birth. Her response to Cathy's attempt to confide in her the mystery and depth of her love for Heathcliff can only elicit the conventional: 'If I can make any sense of your nonsense, Miss . . . it only goes to convince me that you are ignorant of the duties you undertake in marrying.' And in face of Cathy's delirium she can only command, 'Give over that baby-work!' Her rather acid summary of Heathcliff's state of mind is: 'He might have had a monomania on the subject of his departed idol; but on every other point his wits were as sound as mine.' The effect of all these comments is to remove our sympathy for a time from Nelly to the other person, though we never lose our liking for her. Nelly is superstitious and fearful, happy with the normal and ordinary. It is a measure of the normality of the love of Catherine and Hareton that Nelly understands and approves of it.

And, in comparing the reactions of Hindley and Edgar to the loss of their respective wives, she suggests one way of looking at life: 'Linton . . . displayed the true courage of a loyal and faithful soul: he trusted God; and God comforted him. One hoped, and the other despaired: they chose their own lots, and were righteously doomed to endure them.'

She is honest within her limits—'I own I did not like her [Catherine] after she grew up'. It is only at times that her moral and emotional response to what is happening warns the reader not to accept her conclusions.

On the other hand, we have the Calvinistic Methodism of Joseph, which, as in *Shirley*, is linked with hypocrisy. Joseph is 'the wearisomest, self-righteous pharisee that ever ransacked a Bible to rake the promises to himself and fling the curses on his neighbours'. Joseph's insistence on long prayers, sermons, strict Sunday observance, the reading of tracts, is set against his position as tale-bearer and trouble-maker at the Heights, and against his selfish concerns for his own spiritual survival. Joseph's religion is one of superstitious dread of evil and a hatred of the pleasures of life. Nelly's singing of gay hymns or songs is set against his narrow, 'dree' view, 'It's a blazing shaime, ut Aw cannut oppen t'Blessed Book, bud yah set up them glories tuh sattan . . .' When Heathcliff dies, he concludes, 'Th'divil's harried off his soul'.

It is significant that Joseph's religion is always part of, and associated with, life at the Heights. It gives satisfaction to none but Joseph, and can thrive, without affecting anyone else, in the evil ambience of the Heights.

Religion, for the most part, is confined to the idea of reward or punishment after death through heaven and hell, but the major characters generally are just as pleased to reject heaven as we see in Cathy's account of her dream to Nelly: '. . . heaven did not seem to be my home; and I broke my heart with weeping to come back to earth; and the angels were so angry that they flung me out into the middle of the heath on the top of Wuthering Heights; where I woke sobbing for joy.' Hindley indeed blasphemes against God, and Heathcliff only uses His name as an oath. Even Nelly wonders whether 'such people *are* happy in the other world'. Although the spirits of the dead haunt the book, we are never given any real evidence of survival, and generally death is seen as a quiet slumber.

HUMAN NATURE

The only basic and consistent philosophy in the novel is the concern with human nature, and again, it is not the same as

Charlotte's concern. The thesis is presented symbolically in the first pages:

> . . . one may guess the power of the north wind blowing over the edge, by the excessive slant of a few stunted firs at the end of the house; and by a range of gaunt thorns all stretching their limbs one way, as if craving the sun.
>
> Chapter I

Human nature is seen in terms of a natural plant which can be twisted from the norm by the force of an external power. Heathcliff and Hareton are both affected in this way—both are degraded by an external force. And Heathcliff sees the process in the same natural terms: '. . . we'll see if one tree won't grow as crooked as another, with the same wind to twist it!' he says, contemplating the young Hareton, now in his power. But this analogy from nature is not entirely a true one. Nelly remarks later of Hareton that he has 'a mind owning better qualities than his father ever possessed. Good things lost amid a wilderness of weeds, to be sure, whose rankness far over-topped their neglected growth; yet, notwithstanding, evidence of a wealthy soil, that might yield luxuriant crops under other and favourable circumstances.'

And so, basically, human nature cannot be altered, it only *appears* to alter. The roots, the possibilities, cannot be changed. This is Heathcliff's mistake. In seeing Hareton as 'gold put to the use of paving-stones . . . His . . . first-rate qualities . . . are lost' he is ignoring the fact that the quality of the metal cannot be affected by the use it is put to. Thus, Hareton's nature is seen to be fundamentally good, and therefore, while it can be temporarily marred, it cannot be permanently altered for evil. But Heathcliff's nature, although it is affected by outside forces, is fundamentally evil—as a child he is hard, insensible to kindness or to cruelty. Evil and misfortune can twist him permanently by bringing out the evil already in his nature. His son Linton is seen to share this aspect of his father's nature.

Basic also is the feeling that what is evil must finally have an end; Heathcliff's evil passion must burn itself out. No more than the seasons and nature can human nature go on without change, and once the propensity to evil is gone, it will return to the norm of goodness. This is a highly mature (and Shakespearean) notion. It is a view of humanity which cuts through Joseph's talk of God and Satan and Divine intervention and punishment; it ignores social conventions and obligations; it has no concern with the conventional moral code. It is an optimistic view of the human condition, though it also rejects the possibility of any human or divine code offering protection to the vulnerable or eliminating the possible swing to evil.

There is no sense that Emily had to abandon her theory in order to bring her tale to a conclusion, as Charlotte frequently had to. Nor did she need to make comment *on* the action, for the commentary is *in* the action.

THE NATURAL WORLD AND ITS CODE

In one of the essays she wrote for M. Heger, Emily stated: 'Nature is an inexplicable puzzle, life exists on a principle of destruction; every creature must be the relentless instrument of death to the others, or himself cease to live.' The story of Heathcliff is in part a demonstration of this principle of destruction at work in the world of man, though it is taken to the extreme of a demonic-like drive. On the other hand, it is tempered by the demonstration of a complementary drive towards creation and nature's renewal of positive qualities in the love of Catherine and Hareton.

The story of Heathcliff becomes a statement of a certain kind of movement in human affairs, a movement which involves the concepts of good and evil in their general and universal application, as well as in their particular. Though this is a moral theme, we do not find that Emily adopted an allegorical technique to present it as did Charlotte. Charlotte's method is related to the sermon, with its orthodoxy of moral standards and religious beliefs. Emily is dealing with what lies beneath any system of morals or religious beliefs—the fundamental conception of the forces of good and evil as they exist at the levels of nature, of human nature, and the universe.

Generally, therefore, there is little moral implication in the description of character. Whereas Charlotte, simply by describing a person's features, was making a moral judgment, Emily's descriptions tend to be in the direction of relationship to nature, and so morally neutral. Heathcliff is 'a sullen, patient child; hardened, perhaps, to ill-treatment'; Catherine's spirits were 'always at high-water mark', 'A wild, wicked slip she was.' 'Sullenness and patience' are simply natural characteristics. Catherine's 'wickedness' is not evil when seen in the context of 'wildness', and linked with 'slip'—a cutting for grafting or planting. Heathcliff and Edgar, contrasted as 'a bleak, hilly, coal country' and 'a beautiful fertile valley', are not morally contrasted, and if Heathcliff is 'an unreclaimed creature, without refinement, without cultivation: an arid wilderness of furze and whinstone', he is again being seen in terms of nature and natural things.

EXTENSION INTO NATURE

Thus nature and animals of nature are brought in as an extension of human nature; while human nature takes on the aspects of the animal world through metaphor and symbol. Cathy's love for Linton is 'like the foliage in the woods', her love for Heathcliff 'resembles the eternal rocks'. Heathcliff is a fierce, wolfish man who 'gnashes his teeth and foams like a mad dog'. Edgar is a 'sucking leveret', 'a puling chicken', 'a whelp'. Veins boil, tears rain down, faces are clouded, eyes flash and sparkle, abuse pours forth like a deluge, illnesses are weathered. One reviewer comments: 'He [Ellis Bell] appears to think that spiritual wickedness is a combination of animal ferocities, and has accordingly made a compendium of the most striking qualities of tiger, wolf, cur, and wild-cat . . .' Wickedness as seen in human life is linked with characteristic actions and happenings in the animal world, with the additional dimension of being a conscious and not an instinctive drive. There is a strong feeling that whatever happens, however extraordinary and bizarre, is within nature and is therefore 'natural'.

Thus, by means of the imagery, Emily Brontë provides a constant but subterranean commentary on the action which forces us to view it from other than a purely emotional or moral standpoint.

NARRATIVE METHOD

Emily Brontë's narrative method is a complex but skilful one. It is good story-telling to involve the reader immediately in the already chaotic world of the Heights, and as we have shown, the first chapters introduce all the significant aspects of the story with their mystery unexplained. Lockwood is appropriately placed. He comes to things strange as a stranger, and requires an explanation. He takes up a role with which the reader can identify.

Nelly plays a similar role in that, because of her character, incredible events are made to seem credible. A world which can contain a Nelly Dean can contain a Heathcliff, if Nelly Dean says it did.

The two narrators are important, therefore, in terms of drama and of credibility.

In technique, *Wuthering Heights* is a foreshadowing of the more complex novels of Conrad. But Conrad's method derives from the complex moral problem he is dealing with. In *Lord Jim* the moral complexities of Jim's action require many viewpoints and must be placed against the actions of others.

There is something of this in Emily Brontë, but fundamentally the nature of Heathcliff's actions is never open to moral doubt. But the testimony of several narrators—Lockwood, Nelly, Isabella, Joseph, Zillah—is required to convince us of the actuality of events, to show their effects upon a variety of characters, and to place the events within the varied framework of a number of firm and accepted convictions.

It would be wrong, however, to read too much sophistication, too conscious a belief, too subtle a method into the novel. There is no strong evidence that it was Emily Brontë's intention to provide such an appeal to the intellect. The foremost impression of the novel is one of a violent, passionate incident which is told primarily with regard to the age-old concerns of the story-téller, but in which the main character is seen in strong relationship to

the traditional figure of the man possessed by the devil as was
Faust. There is no suggestion, either, that we should draw any
moral from the story; rather the emphasis upon seasonal change,
natural growth, suggests that we look for the instinctive feeling
of the movement from good to evil to good, from calm to passion
to calm, which reflects very strongly the Shakespearean view of
the world. The total absence of authorial commentary reinforces
this.

Selected Bibliography

EDITIONS

Brontë Sisters: Novels & Poems (Wm. Collins Sons & Co., New York).

The novels are also available in The World's Classics edition, published by Oxford University Press, the text of *Wuthering Heights* being Emily's original without Charlotte's emendations; *Jane Eyre* and *Wuthering Heights* are also available in the Penguin Library (Penguin Books, Baltimore, Md.).

C. W. Hatfield: *The Complete Poems of Emily Brontë* (Columbia Univ. Press New York, 1941).

LIFE

E. C. Gaskell: *The Life of Charlotte Brontë* (Oxford Univ. Press, New York).

Winifred Gerin; *Charlotte Brontë: The Evolution of Genius* (Oxford Univ. Press, New York, 1967).

L. and E. M. Hanson: *The Four Brontës* (Shoe String Press, Hamden, Conn., 1949).

Clement Shorter: *Brontës: Life and Letters*, 2 vols. (Haskell House Publishers, New York, 1908).

CRITICAL AND OTHER STUDIES

Charlotte Brontë:

R. B. Heilman: 'Charlotte Brontë's "New Gothic ",' in *From Jane Austen to Joseph Conrad*, ed. R. C. Rathburn and M. Steinmann, Jr. (Univ. of Minnesota Press, Minneapolis, Minn., 1958).

Robert Bernard Martin: *The Accents of Persuasion: Charlotte Brontë's Novels* (W. W. Norton & Co., New York, 1966).

M. H. Scargill: 'All Passion Spent: A revaluation of *Jane Eyre*,' *Univ. of Toronto Quarterly* (January 1950).

Kathleen Tillotson: 'Jane Eyre,' in *Novels of the Eighteen-Forties* (Oxford Univ. Press, New York, 1954).

Emily Brontë:

Arnold Kettle: 'Emily Brontë: *Wuthering Heights,*' in *An Introduction to the English Novel* (Harper & Row, New York).

G. D. Klingopoulos: 'The Novel as Dramatic Poem (II): *Wuthering Heights,*' *Scrutiny* XIV (September 1947).

J. Hillis Miller: 'Emily Brontë' in *The Disappearance of God* (Schocken Books, New York).

Wuthering Heights: Text, Sources, Criticism, ed. Thomas Moser (Harcourt, Brace & World, New York).

Mark Schorer: 'Fiction and the "Analogical Matrix",' in *Critiques and Essays on Modern Fiction,* ed. John W. Aldridge, (Ronald Press, New York, 1952).

Dorothy Van Ghent: 'On *Wuthering Heights,*' in *The English Novel: Form and Fiction* (Rinehart, New York, 1953).

Mary Visick: *The Genesis of Wuthering Heights* (Oxford Univ. Press, New York, 1965).

Both:

Richard Chase: 'The Brontës, or Myth Domesticated,' in *Forms of Modern Fiction,* ed. William Van O'Connor (Indiana Univ. Press, Bloomington, Ind.).

W. A. Craik: *The Brontë Novels* (Barnes & Noble, New York, 1968).

Inga-Stina Ewbank: *Their Property Sphere: A Study of the Brontë Sisters as Early-Victorian Female Novelists* (Harvard Univ. Press, Cambridge, Mass., 1966).

Fannie E. Ratchford, *The Brontës' Web of Childhood* (Russell & Russell, New York, 1964).

Virginia Woolf, *'Jane Eyre and Wuthering Heights,' The Common Reader* (Harcourt, Brace & World, New York).

Index

Main entries are indicated by heavy type